Leading Powerfully From Within

Naomi D. Jones, RN, MS, CRNI

Leading Powerfully From Within©

Naomi D. Jones

ISBN - 13:978-0-692-84615-5

Copyright 2017

Consults Unlimited, Inc.
http://www.lifecoachrn.com/

Editing & Formatting: Lorraine Castle –
Castle Virtual Solutions LLC
http://www.castlevirtualsolutions.com/

Book Cover: Lauren A. Brown –
http://www.labillustration.com/about/

Printed in the United States of America

Dedication

This book is dedicated to my mother, Camilla, who has been and will always remain my inspiration, my teacher and an amazing source of strength.

Acknowledgements

There are so many people I want to thank but, first I must thank God. I thank Him for my life, for His grace and mercy that has allowed me to go through the fires of life and come out on the other side whole and still sane. I am thankful for the inspiration, words and experiences which are in this book.

When it comes to people who were able to see my vision for this book and help me see it to fruition through many stops and starts, my heartfelt thanks go to my husband of over 30 years, Jeff and my main girl Marcia Maddix, RN, MSN. Without the two of them giving me so much support, encouragement and actually being my readers over and over again, this book would not have happened.

I want to thank my editor, Lorraine Castle, who became more of a friend than just a business partner.

Thank you to my sisters, Deborah Hill and Cheryl Chesterfield, for your love and support. To my children Jermaine, Jerell, Jonathan and Jenae, I love you all so much! Let this be an example that you can do anything! To my Aunt Felice who inspires me and all of my family, I love all of you!

Thanks to my longtime friends and supporters Joan Spencer, Louise Nixon, Sherli Allen, Wendy Bruno,

Andrea Stewart and my sisters of Lambda Kappa Mu Sorority Inc.   There are many others who gave a kind word of support and encouragement along the way and to you all, I thank you.

Naomi D. Jones

Foreword

I am especially thrilled, honored and proud to introduce Naomi's literary work to the world. In these times of uncertainty, Naomi's altruistic voice is exactly what leaders need and want to hear. Her sound, reasonable words gives the reader reason to pause, reflect and change. She encourages the reader to find their passion. Leading with passion yields leading with purpose and direction.

The duality of this book is Naomi's God inspired heart to heart message where she addresses the inherent struggles of leadership. She then compels the reader to examine his/her belief systems. The reader is inspired to answer the *Who, What* and *Why* of their lives. Secondly, Naomi gives the reader the *How* (practical application) of leadership.

Naomi openly shares her nursing journey and encourages the reader to consider the next generation of nursing leaders. This book is for leaders (assumed or assigned) in all walks of life. It is for people who desire to live fully through their passion and purpose despite significant obstacles (through the fire).

The best thing about reading this book is it appeals to anyone who aspires to live powerfully from within.

Jeff Jones

Introduction:

Your Journey...It's All Connected

Great Leadership easily starts with a willing heart and a desire to make a difference.
-Mac Anderson-

Most books that teach about leadership principles don't factor in *the inner you.* Without looking within, you will never tap into your true, full potential for success, joy and real power. It also increases the difficulty to make a difference in your life and the lives of others.

The purpose for writing this book is to share some of the knowledge I have gained in over 35 years of nursing, leadership and life. This knowledge has been gained through education and experience. Some of these lessons were learned with great difficulty. I write with the heart of mentorship to assist in developing the next generation of nursing leaders. I am also writing for that person who wants the most out of life. A person who knows somewhere deep inside themselves, that there has to be more to life than just going to work, making money and amassing things.

This book is for the person who is looking for their 'WHY.' The person who knows there is a reason for being here on this earth that's bigger than themselves. Finding your 'why' is all about finding your purpose. Everyone instinctively knows there ***should*** be a purpose or reason for living. Most people get talked out of finding their purpose because they try to fit in. They get bogged down with the status quo and everyday humdrum.

They may have been told, often beginning at a very young age; that they are not important enough, smart enough, or valued enough to even have a purpose. This is often reinforced by people (parents, teachers and peers) and society in general. In an effort to preserve a sense of self (as children and as adults) we often go into survival mode instead of success mode. Survival is when we are operating at our core flight or fight response. At this level, we *react* instead of taking control of our responses to perceived challenges. For some of us, we temporarily get talked out of being powerful and successful, yet we don't feel like '*part of the herd.*' Something keeps pulling at your mind, soul and spirit. Something deep inside says: "I know there's more for me*!*"

How do you figure out what your purpose is and how to manifest it effectively with power? First, by understanding who you are! Real leadership begins with being able to lead yourself. Without proper introspection and alignment of your mind, body, soul and spirit, you can't truly know yourself. It will be difficult, at best, to build vision, sustain focus, make the best decisions or give and receive appropriate guidance. All these factor into having the greatest success possible.

Throughout my career, I learned **how** to love what I do as a nursing leader. I became a better leader because I came to the place of understanding who I am. I recognize how my career fits into my life purpose and I comprehend the privilege and power that is available as a nursing leader.

On my journey I took time to learn about the inner me by examining my past beliefs and viewing them in light of my ambitions and focus of that present time; making the choice – whether those perceptions are still serving me – or if they had become an obstacle to my growth as a self-actualized human being.

After reading this book, I want you to walk away, enlightened and empowered within, by getting to know and understand yourself better – to the point of not only *finding* your **purpose** but *living it* passionately while *creating* a *legacy* of leadership. As nursing leaders, we can grow into the type of leaders who can provide mentorship in a way that's impactful in the present and the future. Enhance your understanding of leadership. Discover how to create a strategy that will help you live your life fully and courageously with joy!

Learn to live as a powerful leader from within. Leave a legacy for future generations. Make an impact in the lives of those you touch!   Live your purpose in a way that will transform them *and* **you forever**.

Contents

SECTION ONE

THE INNER YOU

The Power of Relationship

Life is all about relationships. We don't live in a bubble. Studies have shown that who you spend the most time with is a reflection of who you consider yourself to be. Our relationships can be used as a mirror if we are willing to consider what it shows us about ourselves. Most of our comprehension of who we are is on the surface. There is also the subconscious level where deeper beliefs dictate our actions and behaviors which are unbeknown to us.

Surprisingly, one relationship that we don't examine often is the one we have with ourselves. We don't take time to examine the stories we tell ourselves about how and why we perceive the world and others as we do. We don't look at the conversations we repeat to ourselves over and over. We begin to accept those conversations as truth as to who we are or who we think we appear to be.

There are many factors that influence a person's perceptions. Some factors could come from beliefs they have formed from past experiences and relationships. These opinions are usually formed in our childhood and are reinforced throughout our formative years.

These views also influence the way we think about ourselves and see other people's perception of us. A person with a tendency to be controlling may feel that's 'just the way they are!' The person whose controlling behavior is resulting from fear will often perceive others are trying to control them. They may not even realize how their need to control may affect others in a negative manner. There are many other ways our perceptions are manifested i.e. anger, use of humor, and rebellion to name a few.

Beliefs and emotions drive actions! A possible driver could be fear due to the experience or perception of abandonment. Lack of trust would then be a factor if they decided that people could not be trusted with their best interest. These underlying beliefs motivate us to respond to situations, circumstances and people in a specific way. We have the opportunity to change them if they are not serving us well in fulfilling the desires of our hearts.

When obstacles block us from becoming that person we desire to be (our best self), how do we identify them? Some of those blocks are buried in our subconscious and are not easy to uncover. More so, when we identify and overcome the barriers, how do we replicate the success when new obstacles occur?

What is driving your decisions and behaviors? The need to feel important? Powerful? Needed? Are you feeling rejection? Abandonment? Or is it the desire to love and/or be loved? These drivers can create limited success or blocks for you in your endeavor to reach your highest potential. How do you maneuver around these potential obstacles, get your needs met *and* show up as a powerful person in your life? Your success depends on your ability to understand and interpret your drivers.

As we continue growing internally and incorporate the lessons we learn about ourselves, transformation occurs. Self- discovery includes the process of finding your, who, what and why? Who are you? What do you want for your life? Why are you here? And for inner growth, we need to ask, what has made you who you are today and what do you need to keep or change so you can enjoy your journey in this life?

As you continue reading this book, I will share with you some *guiding principles* of utilizing insight to direct your transformation. I've learned that these principles will assist you in the process of self-discovery of your inner you. When you understand these principles, it becomes easier to work through obstacles when they show up. You will see patterns in your life and can strategize a plan to overcome ones that don't work for you and embrace the ones that do. This is the process for finding and building up the leader within your mind, body, soul and spirit. It is about your relationship with yourself. When you bring your best leader from within to any relationship, whether you are a parent, friend, family member or you are in a leadership position in your career, you have the privilege and the power to transform the lives of others while you live your own life to the fullest.

The journey of transformation is impossible without change. If you want to live a successful life, one that's empowering, satisfying and joyful, then you are in the right place. Let's begin the journey to help you examine where you are right now, visualize your desired future and develop a strategy using some guiding principles to align your thinking with your actions. The following story illustrates some of these principles of insight and transformation.

There's So Much More To Life

There was a little boy who found an eagle's nest in the woods. He decided to take one of the eggs back to his home on the farm. He placed the egg under one of the hens who nurtured the egg until it hatched. When the eagle was born, she lived among the chickens and was raised as a chicken. She learned all the chicken ways but whenever she looked up at the sky and saw eagles flying, she felt a longing to fly with them. She was experiencing the idea of desiring more for her life. Whenever the eagle expressed that feeling to the other chickens they would say things like, "You're dreaming!" "You can't do that!" "It's impossible!" or "You think you're better than us?" Sometimes she even said those things to herself believing them to be true. The eagle tried to quell that yearning for something more and worked hard to fit in. She was living a life that was small, frustrating and with limited joy! The truth is, this eagle was not living to her full potential. She was not living in her purpose!

One day the eagle stepped out on her desires and attempted to fly. She had a few bumps, bruises and setbacks but soon she began to feel empowered. The eagle transformed her thoughts and behaviors. She took some time to find and listen to her inner voice, understand her purpose, and develop a strategy to make her dreams a reality. She connected her powerful leader within to her

*actions and was able live the life she was destined to live!
She was able to fly! She was finally where she belonged.*

This story is for those who recognize that they are an eagle. You are not meant to live a 'chicken' existence. You have a leader within you that **knows** there is more for your life. You have been listening to the other 'chickens' tell you that "You can't be a leader". or "You can't care about people because they can't be trusted to support you" or "It's impossible to get power and influence without playing dirty!"

When you fight for positive transformation, you may hear some say, "You think you're better than us?" The truth is, your desires, dreams and vision are bigger and better than what they can see for you and maybe even for themselves! You *know,* you are not satisfied with your present situations and circumstances. You **know** you have a purpose!

GUIDING PRINCIPLE-#1

YOU CAN CHANGE THE TRAJECTORY OF YOUR LIFE RIGHT NOW AS YOU LEARN THE PROCESS OF SELF-LEADERSHIP. IF YOU WANT SOMETHING DIFFERENT YOU HAVE TO DO SOMETHING DIFFERENT. TAKING AFFIRMATIVE ACTION WILL SHIFT EVERYTHING AROUND YOU INCLUDING YOU.

I was that eagle trapped in the chicken coup. Growing up in one of the largest public housing projects in North America, I always had that inner spirit that said, "There's got to be more than just growing up, going through trials and tribulations only to have it end in death."

The eagle in me said: I *know* I there's a reason I'm here on this earth. I have something to offer in this world and to do it I need to believe that I can fly. I also had to examine what was holding me back from believing I could fly.

My perceptions of who I was in this world as a young black girl was challenged by society, my peers and sometimes the adults in my life. I grew into what I perceived as a supposedly comfortable space in my life. I wouldn't try to be special. I tried to not appear too smart. It would never work for long. I wanted success yet I questioned, what was different in me from other successful people who were winning at life?

Through many trials I had to figure out that success comes with challenges and is surrounded by risk and potential failure. I assessed the backgrounds of my perceptions and realized that there is no difference between me and successful people except the will to do the work of understanding and embracing my gifts, talents and purpose.

During those eagle-in-a-chicken-coup moments, I would *assess* my situation, make a decision about it and take action. It always changed the trajectory of my life in that moment. That process is ongoing and creates the 'journey' of life. The strategies of insight, acceptance and self-leadership led to my rewards of being able to fly. I believe that you have that eagle too! In every instance where you find that you are not where you want to be, assess, make a decision and take action. We have *freedom of will* to *choose* how we *act* and respond to life's circumstances.

What Do I Know?

In my life there have been countless opportunities to develop insight and skills of transformation. For intent and purposes of this book, I will connect those lessons learned through my nursing career as a leader.

I have been in nursing for over 35 years with more than 20 years in management. I have seen the good, the bad and the ugly side of nursing. Sometimes the ugly was so bad it made me completely understand the phrase, ***"Nurses Eat Their Young."*** Sometimes I would wonder why I even came back to work the next day! Sadly, I've had too many of those days! For those who are not nurses, this phrase speaks to nurses not being as caring toward each other as they are to their patients.

In my career, I have come to know that everyone in a leadership position doesn't belong there. There are those who get into leadership positions, find out it's not for them and get out. Then there are those who stay, but shouldn't. They may stay for the bump in salary or sometimes feel ashamed to leave because it would show others they really "couldn't hack it." The ones who stay for those reasons have an attitude that leads to defensiveness and ineffectiveness. In fairness, most of us were never formally trained to be nursing leaders. We often had to "figure it out." How do you open the door and train the next generation of nursing leaders when you are barely keeping your own head above water?

There were many legitimate reasons why nursing leaders feel that the job is overwhelming at times i.e. lack of support, lack of authority, bullying, racism, sexism and excessive workload. However, there was a reality that existed where on some levels we are unprepared for the role. I've spoken to so many nursing leaders over the years who quietly but honestly tell me they too are living the *"imposter syndrome."*[i] That's where they feel they were not adequately prepared for their roles in leadership and they may have had idealistic expectations about themselves as leaders. This is usually manifested by overworking, anxiety, use of charm, self-doubt and avoiding accountability for their own decisions.

These people have skills but also have hidden fear in the back of their mind that it will be discovered how much they don't know – which eats at their confidence. Without confidence, some become bullies to hide their insecurities, while others may shrink from their responsibilities hoping to be "liked" because they are uncomfortable in their abilities.

Comparatively, others, like me, found comfortable areas within my own expertise. In this space, I could excel in my abilities and stayed away from areas where I had less confidence. Occasionally, I found myself listening to other people trying to convince me that I wasn't 'qualified' to be a leader. Worse yet, at times, I had those same doubts. Often this limited my ability to grow both professionally and personally. None of these styles work when it comes to being an effective leader.

In today's healthcare environment, so many managers are *frustrated, disappointed and overwhelmed.* It may seem as though we don't have time to help others. Many other nursing leaders try to do a good job but feel unappreciated, and think about getting out of management. They struggle to balance their personal need with the needs of the organization. These stressors, if unchecked, lead to frustration and burnout which cause many nurses to leave this career choice.

In spite of these limitations, I learned and adapted. I tried to make things work using learned leadership theories like leadership styles i.e. Laissez-Faire, Transformational and Autocratic. I tried to figure out which style fit me and those around me. These theories did help me gain some insight into my leadership style, yet it was not enough to sustain real change.

We rarely examine the reason "why" people have those styles. Just knowing these types of leaders exist is not enough to change the way nurses treat themselves and each other. There are underlying factors that cause people to adopt "styles" to cover up what's driving their behavior. This "mask" that people hide behind gives rise to the bullying that goes on in the nursing community.

Some of the bullies were my managers who were making my life miserable as they masked their own insecurities. The worst part is, without introspection on their part, they may not have even realized the cause or effect of how they impacted their colleagues and staff.

Thank goodness, I also had some managers, directors and CEO's who were awesome. They found the secret of balance, embraced the ideals of self-leadership in their own lives and knew how to pour some of that experience into my life (for which I am forever grateful)! When it was my turn to step into leadership, it was my passion to make a positive impact in the nurses' lives I would encounter. It was equally important to maintain the dignity and integrity of being a nurse leader. It was not easy! What I discovered was that you just can't **will** yourself into being a powerful effective leader. You need some basic understanding of the inner you and strategies to effectively use that new knowledge.

Passion and Purpose

GUIDING PRINCIPLE #2

WHATEVER YOU DO HAS TO BE AN EXPRESSION OF YOUR UNIQUENESS (PASSION) AND IT MUST MAKE SOMEONE ELSE'S LIFE BETTER (PURPOSE).

You and I absolutely have a purpose for being here. So many people do not know their passion or purpose. The fact is your passion can be found in your uniqueness. What's special about you? Sometimes this is hidden because we have decided to become part of the herd and not let our inner light shine. We are afraid of not belonging. The truth is, where you belong is living *your* purpose. As the guiding principle states, purpose is directly related to helping others. Your passion is your unique place in how that gets done.

I love helping people through connection and conversation. I was always in trouble in school for talking. However, I discovered my gift is in connecting with people through conversation. Nursing turned out to be the greatest career for me to live my passion and my purpose. On my journey, I discovered writing is another expression of my passion and purpose. What is yours?

What I've discovered, is that you must take the time to reflect on your life's passion and purpose. You must take account of the story you tell yourself about who you are. Where did that story come from? You might just be talking yourself out of your passion due to some hidden drivers. Decide what's working and what's not working in your story to direct the change you want to see. Otherwise, you're just going through the motions of living a life that's going nowhere fast.

GUIDING PRINCIPLE -#3

THERE ARE MANY PASSIONS ONE CAN HAVE IN LIFE BUT THERE IS REALLY ONE PURPOSE.

Starting out in life, most people do not have a clue about their passion or their purpose. There are so many ways to serve in the world. Some people have a gift working with children. Some have a gift and passion for business. Some have a talent of strategizing and have a passion for the military. You need to find what works for you. Initially I wasn't sure of my passion. One thing I knew was that I wanted to help people even in the smallest of situations.

Everyone instinctively feels there *should* be a purpose or reason for living. There *is* a reason that you were born in this day and time. Interest can lead you to your passion. Talent can also lead you to your passion. When you can enjoy your career, it's easier to be creative, joyful and excited to tap into your personal power from within. Passion on your journey can direct you to your purpose. It's easier when you have a process on how to become clear about your purpose. I've developed a meaningful, implementable process that will help you get that understanding of your purpose. It's called the *"Lead*

With Power Blueprint." This is a formula I've created that will help guide you toward discovery of your purpose and will be discussed in greater detail shortly.

After you become clear about your why (passion), the manifestation of that "why" is the next step (purpose). Being a leader (your career) is one way to manifest your purpose. You bring your essence (who you are) into your relationships which plays a huge part in what comes out of those relationships. When you are not fully engaged with yourself, you will decrease the impact on the relationships around you. As you grow toward fulfillment of your highest self, you move into the realm of becoming extraordinary. People who decide to live life through their passion and purpose can create amazing circumstances and situations for others.

You are a person designed to leave an impact in this world! You chose to put yourself in a leadership position of power and influence. Does your career encompass your passion? You accepted the premise that you will lead and manage other people. Having more to life with passion and purpose is not only for yourself. When you have more, you can give more! Leadership is a position of privilege and purpose! This is also true when you become a parent, teacher, friend or any other position that puts you in a relationship with another human being.

Living Purposefully With Passion

What do you do with passion and purpose?

Helping others is the epitome of our existence on a physical and spiritual level.

Mark 12:31b (KJV)

...Thou shalt love thy neighbor as thyself. There is none other commandment greater than these.

This is echoed in many other faiths. When you love others as yourself you can empathize with others even if you are not in their exact situation or circumstance. You would never wish the worst of things for yourself so why would you accept negative things for others? Herein lies a piece for introspection. Are you accepting of "less than" for others because there is an underlying story you tell yourself about you? At your core do you feel less than? Do you believe you *"made it"* alone so why can't others? There are many versions of these scenarios but if you can get to the point you believe in the best for yourself, you must believe the best should be available to all!

Self-actualization is the goal of our human existence on physical and emotional levels. Maslow's Hierarchy of Needs Theory[ii] suggests the hierarchy of needs is vital to every human being. We all have physiological needs, which is a priority for all people (air, food and water). His theory states that if those needs aren't met, then you really can't reach the next level of

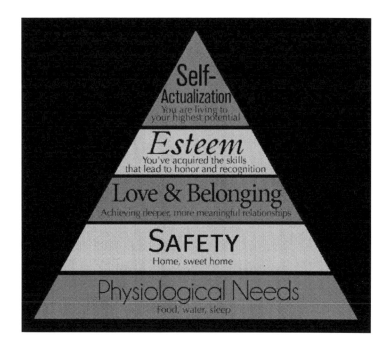

achievement which is safety. The process is the same in moving through all of the levels.

In getting these needs met, our goal is to become our best self. Why? I submit the purpose of being your best self is so you are able to help others. It is our job to create winning situations.

In life, I've always had compassion for the underdog. Growing up in the heart of the civil rights movement and the women's movement, I understand what disenfranchisement feels like. The truth is all human beings undergo some sort of adversity or challenges in varying degrees no matter your upbringing. Love and belonging are right after safety in this theory. If we as leaders utilize this theory in our practice, we will be meeting most people here. We can help meet needs at this level by creating work teams. We then can attempt to help them reach esteem and recognition through mentoring, coaching and coordinating meaningful work. Finally we can point them in the direction of self-actualization as we reach for it ourselves in our own journey.

GUIDING PRINCIPLE-#4

INTROSPECTION IS AN ART AND A SCIENCE. TIME, FOCUS, HONESTY AND COMPASSION FOR ONE'S SELF ARE NECESSARY FOR TRUE INTROSPECTION. THEN YOUR DESIRES AND/ OR BLOCKS TO PERSONAL SUCCESS CAN BECOME CLEARER.

These revelations of self, allow you the opportunity to see and build up the leader within. Your vision, purpose and passion become clearer when you have a better perception about who you are inside. Introspection requires that you take time for yourself. So often we are so busy that we actually strive to "get back in the game" after any setback. These are the actual times we should slow down and assess the impact on our lives from the setback. We must honestly look at what happened, why it happened and what are the other potential outcomes that would have been available if we had made different choices. Sometimes there may not be anything we could have changed but there may be a different way you can choose to perceive the situation.

Your relationships with yourself and others will blossom and you will reap the rewards of transformation when you assimilate the lessons of your life. As a leader in your own life, you must have vision, gather necessary information, strategize a plan, implement it, evaluate it and adjust as needed. Whether or not you are in a management position right now you will benefit from the principles of introspection. Some of the benefits are: peace, confidence, joy, patience, resilience, compassion and POWER!

The Art of Transformation and Transitions

GUIDING PRINCIPLE - #5

YOUR JOURNEY IS MADE UP OF TRANSITIONS BUT WHAT'S REALLY NEEDED IS TRANSFORMATION.

Transitions

Perception of who you are is directly related to how you view the transitions in your life. When I considered how my leadership skills developed, I began to see patterns of transitions and transformations. Transitions occur all the time throughout our lives. According to Merriam-Webster Dictionary, transition is a noun and a verb indicating action. To transition is: an act or the process of passing from one state, stage or place, or subject to another to make a change from one state, place, or condition to another.

It's like the transition of eyeglasses that change to a tint when exposed to sunlight and return to clear when sunlight is decreased or going from one job to another. Linguistically, transitions within sentences help guide the reader from one logical thought to another. Transitioning also happens in the mind. In our journey of life we go through transitions constantly. We are always changing our position, thoughts and actions due to our perception of the moment. As leaders we can help our staff transition into their staff roles. Transitions may or may not be permanent. Transitioning is a process of its own and does not always lead to transformation.

Transitions make up our "journey." We transitioned from regular citizens to nurses. In nursing school, we learned about the science of life and health. We also learned about the art of nursing which incorporated the mental, emotional and physical needs of the human body and spirit. We acquired knowledge about how magnificently the body works right down to minutia of atoms, cells and DNA. Graduation indicated a transition period had ended for those who were able to assimilate the knowledge, thinking and culture of nursing. The nature of transition is that as one stage ends another begins.

The next transition came after graduation and you are on your way to work. A new transition was beginning from student to professional. Remember that feeling of trepidation even if you were an 'A' student? As you worked, you had opportunities to transition from neophyte to competence through matching your knowledge, mindset, competency and confidence to actual experience.

Transitional periods, therefore, must include the *ability to practice* the right skills enough to build both competence and confidence. Transitional periods may leave you exhausted, irritable and can be an emotionally challenging process. It's uncomfortable because new skills must be not only obtained but *mastered.*   It's a period of growth, of changing, of becoming something new.

During any time in a transitional period a person may choose to close themselves off from moving forward. Some may decide that they have become comfortable in a certain space and refuse to continue toward transformation. Others become stuck. We must always be aware of these periods when growth can stagnate if our desire is true transformation. Insight into transitional periods are the pre-requisite in the journey toward transformation.

Transformations

GUIDING PRINCIPLE-#6

TRANSFORMATION OCCURS WHEN YOU KNOW WHO YOU ARE IN RELATION TO YOUR MIND, BODY, SOUL AND SPIRIT.

Transformation is to change in appearance, nature or character – to metamorphose like a caterpillar morphs into a butterfly. True transformation occurs in the mind, body, soul and spirit. It's when you *"get it!"* It's when a new you emerges. Now you live it, breathe it and it becomes like part of your DNA.

Transformation as a nurse was manifested as you began thinking, feeling and acting like a nurse instinctively. You became able to look at a patient and know that something is about to go wrong, even before you could put a name to it. That's when you've arrived in the transformation nation of nurses.

As nursing leaders, we need to be life learners. Healthcare and technology are always changing as are leadership concepts. This information brings value to your ability to make sound decisions accurately and timely. What will add to your ability to lead effectively is the ongoing development of the inner you. Your perceptions should always be evaluated in your decision making process. This will keep you from making decisions based on emotions or other pressures.

The *art* of transformation occurs in the *reconciliation* and *integration* of your mind, body, soul and spirit. To transform, we need to take time, like the caterpillar, reconciling the pain, joy, mistakes, and successes, so we can come out stronger than before. Transformation brings the balance, the equilibrium, the homeostasis of our human existence.

Creating Change Through Transformation

One thing that I've learned is that life is full of challenges. Change is one of those challenges. We have all heard the phrase that "Change is constant." Usually when we hear it, it's because you, as a nursing leader, must implement something you really may not fully grasp or believe in and it needs to happen immediately! The reality is change is constant but we can learn to flow with the dynamics of change when we are prepared for it.

Most of us seek to change the people, places and things outwardly around us to make ourselves appear better. We may fire staff or depend on your more proficient staff to get the work done while allowing mediocre staff to just exist. These acts may appear to fix some problems but will not lead to a positive, open place where everyone has the opportunity to grow and enhance their journey to transformation.

To be a successful leader we must look within to exact change. Inner change includes looking for those unnoticeable patterns we have developed to get us from one point to another in life. Effective leadership within will occur when you combine the mental, emotional, physical and spiritual components of your life and internalize the knowledge of who you are inside. Build your knowledge into wisdom. Wisdom is applied knowledge which is necessary to make the best decisions in work and life, to be able to give good guidance and have the greatest success possible.

Without choosing sustainable inner change, we revert to old ways of emotionally spending a lot of energy fighting never-ending battles for small victories. As you transform into that 'new person' you have the *choice* to not remain in that old state. The bottom line is you must make the moment by moment choice to tap into your inner you. If not, you won't get the joy or success or sense of fulfilment you're really looking for.

Freedom Through Transformation

> ### GUIDING PRINCIPLE-#7
>
> ### FREEDOM OCCURS WHEN YOU CAN BE BALANCED. THIS IS THE BEGINNING OF GAINING CONTROL OF YOUR DESTINY.

You have chosen to be a leader as part of your career. It is imperative to be balanced in all aspects of our mind, body, soul and spirit to be an effective leader. Is your approach to balance working? We all develop patterns in how we react to life experiences, circumstances and situations. Some of those patterns cause us to act in certain *predictable* ways. Sometimes those very patterns stop us from flying as an eagle. Other times they can weigh you down just enough that you may fly but you won't be above the fray!

You must really understand how you operate internally. When you purposely lead and manage your thoughts, behaviors, emotions, and predictable reactions, you can then choose your response in a more positive and fulfilling way that will *first* bless you and then others.

In nursing, we must reconcile the medications at the end of each shift. This just means that you counted the pills (usually narcotics) with a nurse from the previous shift. Then knowing and documenting who received those medications during your shift, account for how many pills are left then reconcile with the nurse from the shift following you.

Our present is a collection of our yesterdays. Who we are in the future will include how we perceive what happens to us today. We must acknowledge the past, document where we are today and then reconcile our mind, body, soul and spirit to give the correct accounting to the *'next shift'* in our journey.

This method will allow you to let go of past negatives, embrace the present by making conscious choices and reach for the future in renewed strength, hope and anticipation. We grow internally by "taking a checkup from the neck up" every now and again. The more often you do it, the more you will become a most effective leader for the most important person...YOU!

Creating freedom through transformation in your life is to gain mastery over your *mind, body, soul and spirit.* It is a skill and process that's absolutely, necessary if you want to lead yourself powerfully from within. Frustration comes when your life is imbalanced. The mind, body, soul and spirit complement each other. Alignment is crucial in obtaining a balanced life. When our mind, body, soul and spirit is balanced, you find joy and peace even when external events may be topsy-turvy in your life and or career.

The next most important concept to set yourself free is realizing that **life is a journey!** It's an ongoing process of learning and growing. It's about change, both externally and internally. It's about becoming better, more effective and using what you learn to become a positive influence in this world. It's a process that happens continually. It's also about making decisions and mistakes, and having forgiveness and compassion for yourself. It's about building a legacy from within that leaves your positive imprint on the people whose lives you touch. That includes your family, friends, patients, staff and co-workers. Maya Angelou so eloquently said:

> *"I've learned that people will forget what you said, people will forget what you did, but people will never forget how you made them feel."* ~ *Maya Angelou*[iii]

You can make an impact on the lives you touch but one must have the **will** to make that impact a positive one. Life is like a pool table. The pool stick and the cue ball are used to move the other balls around the table by connecting with them through impact. As we move through this journey of life, we are the cue ball. We touch the lives of many who then touch other lives and so on. This is how you build your legacy, one person, one relationship and one moment at a time.

Purpose vs Self

GUIDING PRINCIPLE- #8

CHOOSING EMPATHY AND COMPASSION IS HOW WE BEGIN MAKING A DIFFERENCE IN SOMEONE ELSE'S LIFE.

You have the choice to make necessary decisions deliberately but with empathy. Empathy allows you to avoid negative emotions that could possibly influence your actions to create an unfair outcome. Leadership is about you but it's not *all* about you. Empathy and compassion starts from within. It's a choice to try and see someone else's side of an issue – to try and see a different perspective.

Developing insight into your own perceptions will help you become more empathetic. Empathy does not mean you agree with everyone but it will help you bring understanding to any relationship you have. It's how we 'show up' in our lives. Empathy begins with realizing that you become a powerful leader so you can influence positive outcomes for others. What does that mean? You are powerful as you allow others to stand powerful in their experience of life.

GUIDING PRINCIPLE- #9
IT'S ALL ABOUT YOU BUT IT'S
NOT ALL ABOUT YOU!

It's about you! You must be a priority in your own life! You need to train your mind, nurture your soul, take care of your body and embrace your spirit. When you do, you will be able to build and sustain your inner strength, embody your vision, have fortitude, focus, healthy boundaries and effectiveness. Why do you need these attributes? So, you can smoothly make decisions using your internal compass instead of being influenced by circumstances. Situations will no longer dictate your reactions. Your purpose will keep you grounded. Mindfulness is a tool to help you maintain focus on your passion and vision. Taking time to be aware of what's going on internally is key to tapping into the inner you.

It's not all about you! You are in a position of service. That's the real purpose of leadership – to lead others! Now, I'm not talking about titles only. Leaders light the way for others so they too can enjoy the light. When you think about it, you can lead in any situation, at any given time. Leading is often done by modeling behavior that you want another person to emulate. People will watch you long before they listen to you. You purposefully make the choice to take charge of your mind, body, soul and spirit to influence an outcome. As a leader, this skill is priceless. It begins with you! Being in charge of yourself builds confidence. Confidence in yourself helps yield benevolence to others. Empathy can live in this space because you are operating in your purpose. When it all comes together, everyone wins!

Giving vs Self-Care

GUIDING PRINCIPLE-#10

YOU CAN'T GIVE WHAT YOU DON'T HAVE!
SELF-CARE IS A PRIORITY.

We are taught as children that we should not be self-absorbed. As nurses, we generally have an exaggerated sense of just the opposite. Nursing is the profession that encompasses patience, compassion, empathy and caring. We are judged by how these characteristics show up in our actions to our patients. How often have you heard a patient or another nurse say, "Oh! She's such a good nurse!" It's usually when a nurse is going out of her way to exhibit one or more of these qualities. 'Good' is associated with what we physically do for our patients along with the empathy and compassion we show them. If we as nurses believe these are good qualities to exhibit, why don't we model them for ourselves and our peers?

As nurses, we came to this profession because we felt we have something to give to others. We desire to help people live to their fullest potential by helping them manage their health. We can live one aspect of our highest potential by doing the work we do. But, what about us as individuals? I can't tell you how often I've had conversations with colleagues that end with, "I don't have work/ life balance or time for myself." Yet they will take any extra time they do find and give it to other people.

They are living a contradiction. If they stop long enough for some reflection and make themselves a priority along with some principles outlined in this book and the blueprint, they will be able to change the trajectory of their work /life balance.

As nurses, in general, we are caring, competent and compassionate. Beginning with our training to become nurses, we are taught the patient's needs come first. When I began nursing school, PM care (care given in the evening to patients) included back rubs (I may be dating myself), smoothing out the sheets (no wrinkles, which could cause skin breakdown) and almost singing the patient a lullaby (not really). We are taught to care for the "whole" person including their mental, physical, emotional and spiritual needs.

We were and still are trained to anticipate and elevate the needs of our patients to facilitate their healing. Sometimes, to meet those needs, we serve at our own expense (working short staffed, mandatory overtime, inappropriate staff-patient ratios and increased workloads.) What has become clear to me is: the care we have for our patients is often not extended to ourselves or our peers.

This self-deprivation philosophy has to stop! Why do so many nurses experience burn out? Because we are trying to give what we don't have! We need to show ourselves patience, compassion, empathy, and kindness strategically and purposefully first; then give to others. As they say on airplanes, "Put your own oxygen mask on first; then help others!"

Selfishness vs Altruism

When you really think about how to care for others before yourself (altruism); that speaks to how most nurses act in their role. We work under complicated and stressful conditions. We work with limited resources, difficult staff – patient ratios, become exposed to many life-threatening diseases, emotional abuse, physically work long hours (standing, pulling, lifting), and mental stress. We also don't usually have the time to even empty our bladders on a regular basis!

We are the official and unofficial watchdog of all other healthcare personnel. For those of you who are not nurses, it is the nurse who oversees the aide in providing personal care, the pharmacy (were the right medications sent), the physician (did he /she order the right tests, medications etc.) and the list goes on...

The problem with this level of altruism is that most nurses put any care of themselves at the bottom of the list. As nursing leaders, we add another level of care with staff to our already long list, pushing ourselves even further down the list.

Leadership is when we live our lives in service to others, unselfishly, for the greater good. Leadership *doesn't* mean you cannot care about yourself! The good news is *unselfish* doesn't mean you can't put yourself first. The greater good of others does not mean you have no right to benefit from that good. Living life in service does not mean that you have to be a doormat! Leadership doesn't have to hurt! For better distinction, some definitions need to be challenged.

The definition for *selfish* as per the dictionary is:
- Devoted to or caring *only* for oneself; concerned *primarily* with one's own interests, benefits, welfare, etc. *regardless* of others.
- Characterized by or manifesting concern or care *only* for oneself.

We have been taught to not be selfish, especially as little girls, from childhood (not that it was totally wrong but I believe we have taken it too far). Though altruism is a wonderful attribute, I would like to tweak this definition for our intent and purposes. First, we are going to remove the word *"only"* and we're going to replace *regardless* with *"including concern."* When you do that the definition changes drastically!
Let's read it again;
- Devoted to or caring for oneself; concerned with one's own interests, benefits welfare, etc. *including* concern for others.
- Characterized by or manifesting concern or care for oneself

When you read it now, it really describes the attributes of "self-care." As nursing leaders, we need to care for ourselves and there is nothing wrong with being concerned about your own welfare and our own interests. This is the healthiest way to live when we balance it with a concern for others. Being totally unselfish doesn't make sense either. Understanding your goals, your worthiness to be seen and heard along with acknowledgement of clear boundaries, help balance our definition of selfish vs unselfish. The definition for ***unselfish*** is:

> ➤ Not selfish; disinterested; generous; altruistic.

What's interesting about this definition of unselfishness is the word "disinterested" in self. How does this attitude affect you not only as a leader but as an individual? If you are *disinterested* in your own values, your own vision or your own purpose, you will not live a full life that brings *you* joy and fulfillment. Well, the truth is, you will get glimpses of that joy and fulfillment but it will be difficult to sustain. Your life is about you having interest in obtaining abundance for yourself so that it ***overflows*** to others impacting them for the better.

There are times when you should be more selfish (our definition) or unselfish (also our definition). Acknowledging the value of wisdom and understanding begins the process! You can live a life that's selfishly unselfish with love and resilient leadership!

Balance here is the key! Here are 4 tips on creating a process for balance in your life.

➢ Take inventory of what you are doing with your time. Are you running around with increasing job requirements, deadlines, children's activities and family obligations? STOP! Take a moment and just list them on a piece of paper. Reflect on what you do over one week's time. What do you see? Take time for this exercise over a few weeks. Give yourself time to explore your thoughts, feelings and emotions. It will give you increased clarity when you prioritize what to let go.

➢ Begin introducing yourself to yourself! Write down the things you like to do (You may have to think back to before having children or the job). Write those things down, no matter how small they might be. Again take time to reflect.

➢ Begin the reconciliation. For us to be our best and be complete, we must reconcile our mind, body, soul and spirit. We need to match up our total being with life's demands. Create a list acknowledging all the things you do for others. Then eliminate a task entirely, share the responsibility of it, or completely delegate it to someone else (possibly the person you are doing it for).

➢ Next, take your list of things you enjoy and begin to transition one thing from your personal enjoy list into your life on a regular basis. Continue this process until you achieve balance.

Patients look to nurses as their advocates. As nursing leaders, your staff looks to you for guidance and care. Your families look to you as a resource for everything that goes on in their lives. If you REALLY care about them, you absolutely must put yourself first. You will be able to improve patient care by improving your self-care. You will improve the quality of your life if you take the time to advocate and care for yourself. YOU ARE WORTH IT!

SECTION TWO

MIND, BODY, SOUL AND SPIRIT

Blueprint For Self-Discovery

I have created a process to address this improper order of care. We must change the order of things to reflect ourselves as a priority, then family/friends, peers/staff then patients. I have created a process to help take care of the leader in you. I have taken the concept of the nursing care plan...yes, the care plan and created the *"Lead With Power Blueprint"* to help you find and live your purpose by first becoming aware of and supportive of yourself.

The care plan is a basic process we learned in nursing school. Assess, design intervention, evaluate outcomes, reassess for improvement and adjust as needed. The care plan governs everything that's done in nursing. It helps mold your thinking to the point that it becomes second nature. For those who are nurses you may not even write care plans for your patients any longer but I guarantee if you examine closely what you do, you are still operating the tenets of care planning. The first phase of designing a care plan is assessment. It is where you look to see what's going on especially with your thoughts and to look for patterns. When evaluating your own life, these patterns must be identified and assessed to see if they are serving you or not.

This takes personal commitment, honesty and time if you want to see true transformation in your life. Here are some questions to ask yourself:

> ➤ How do I behave in certain situations? What are my thoughts that are associated

with my behavior? Has my past affected my thoughts and behaviors today? Were you the 'good' or 'problem' child? What were your perceptions around "fitting in?"

➤ What skills did you develop in relationship to your perceived position in your family, community? Are you trusting, dismissive, going out of your way?

➤ What beliefs did you form about the people around you? Could they be trusted? Were they dismissive?

➤ How many of those formed beliefs do you still use today? How are they working for you now?

➤ Can you distinguish between facts and beliefs? Is there a previously held perception that needs to change?

These are areas that require introspective assessment (figuring out what's not working). This is the beginning of making significant advances in obtaining transformation in your life. As a self-leader, utilizing a tool like the "Lead With Power Blueprint," *will* make an impact on the lives you interact with and leave a legacy that will influence the future!

It's going to take a person of strong conviction to utilize the tools and premises outlined in this book but the rewards are endless! In every relationship, you have the choice to leave a positive impact on another and most importantly yourself. You can identify and manage the leader within by being a forever learner of your mind, body, soul and spirit. Learn yourself through the thoughts you have, the choices you make and through keeping track of your vision, identifying your passion and your purpose.

The Journey to Transformation

Lead With Power Blueprint

Remember the components of the Nursing Care Plan, (which we all had strong feelings about) **Nursing Diagnosis, Intervention, Outcome and Evaluation.** Even though we may not have been a fan of care plans, they do have a purpose.

1. They teach us how to assess a problem and give a name to it (Nursing Diagnosis).

2. They give us a standardized way to take in and organize information about a problem.

3. The care plan helps us to focus on specific outcomes we want to obtain.

4. The most important part, Evaluation! The care plan teaches the principles of assessing for success and how to tweak our interventions and refocus if needed.

I have modified the care plan process to reflect the needs of the leader. The principles remain the same. To ensure certain, specific outcomes you must have a process. The *"Lead With Power Blueprint"* is formulated with process principles like the care plan.

Assessment: Introspection Equals The Beginning Of Vision And Wisdom

When we assess, we are evaluating the present situation. We are making a judgement and placing a value on some portions of our past and future and how it relates to our present. The question becomes, do those values relate to the vision I have for myself? Who am I in relationship to myself and others? What's my big picture? For me, simply put; it's being able to help others. My vision is to do that on a big stage. Over the years, as I have become better able to see; that stage became even bigger. Initially my stage was my family and immediate friends. In school, that stage grew, as a nurse, it grew even bigger then continued to grow as a nurse in management and working with many community organizations in my personal life. Now I have become an entrepreneur, speaker, author and mentor. I have become clearer over the years about my purpose and vision by following my values of helping others with love, compassion and integrity balanced with processes and accountability.

Diagnosis Equals Needs

Now that you have a vision, we need to examine the reason we have that vision. On the road to fulfilment according to Maslow's theory we are always on the mission of meeting our needs. Our needs are always in a state of flux. An important fact to know is that we never "arrive." What! The road to self- actualization is paved with challenges. The journey is also paved with great rewards as we experience successes. Those needs drive us to express ourselves through our behaviors. As we grow, we continue to develop our stories about ourselves and our relationship to our environment. In matching our needs and behaviors with our vision and goals mentally, physically and spiritually, we will always be headed in the direction of self-actualization.

Implementation/ Self-care and Evaluation/Connection (Mind, Body, Soul and Spirit). The care plan focuses on opportunities and soul-utions that will increase your ability to have personal fulfillment and joy. By taking specific steps to take care of yourself while you define and achieve *your* goals, this plan makes sure that the care you provide to yourself will transform you into the ***awesome*** individual you are meant to be. As we gain mastery over our mind, body soul and spirit we will better manage our emotions and make better choices to keep us focused on the goal of self-actualization.

Mind, Body, Soul and Spirit: Where Ultimate Transformation Takes Place

The mind, body, soul and spirit is the complete package of who we are. If you want to develop the complete inner you, each of these areas must be studied personally, honorably and with kind-heartedness for self. We are often our own worst critics. It's also an important factor in building your legacy. Here are just a few ways you can begin that process.

The mindset of leadership is service. Leaders are the innovators and translators of vision. Sometimes it's your vision and sometimes it's the vision of others (your organization). As leaders we are in service to the vision and to those who need help to see the vision (our staff and patients). There are two things you must understand and practice to get into alignment with your purpose. You must understand how your brain works and how you can master it by practicing the Art of Mindfulness.

Your Brain

Your brain is a complex, awesome organ. First understand that your brain works in stories. It receives so much information that it needs to make sense of it all. One way it does that is through story. This is why your perceptions become reality for you. "It's just the way I am," is just a version of that story. We make logic of our experiences through story. BUT is your story true? Is it a belief or a fact? There is a distinction. The wonderful thing is we can choose to change our perception of any beliefs we have by changing the story. [iv]

The other major way our brains influence our actions is through our instincts (reptilian), our emotions (limbic) and our very intellect (neurocortex). (Tanzi, n 2013). Are they in balance?

This is what an unbalanced brain looks like:

➤ **Instincts-** Is your fear dominating your actions causing you to fight (be dominant, controlling) or flight (refusing to confront issues)?
➤ **Emotions-** Are your emotions taking the lead? Is your sense of compassion gone? Are you yelling, speaking unkindly, gossiping, nit picking or wearing your heart on your sleeve (crying)?
➤ Does your **intellect** tell you, "I have a job to do and I won't let anyone or anything get in *my* way?" or "I don't need anyone, I can do this alone."

Practicing mindfulness will help put the brain systems in balance. None of these manifestations of your brain's personality is wrong but they only benefit you and those around you when they are in balance. You need to understand what's going on around you and in you. You must connect with your entire self (mind, body, soul and spirit) and manage it. It's about making the choice to be mindful of your internal temperature every moment of the day.

> ➢ **Mindfulness**

Mindfulness is the act of paying attention in a neutral manner, devoid of judgment, assumptions, analysis and calculation. It's about being aware of what's going on with your intellect, your emotions and your instincts. It's also understanding how your story may or may not be influencing your reactions to whatever stimuli is eliciting a response from you. The mindset of practicing mindfulness is when you realize that there are no absolutes and change begins with you. When we are not holding issues in judgment, we can see the forest for the trees. We can see the problem and not necessarily focus on the people involved in the problem.

In the mindset of service, it becomes easier to reflect, put emotions, intellect and instinct in balance and use critical thinking skills to problem solve. It becomes easier to remember we are all human beings in need of guidance and empathy. When your mind is balanced, you will be able to effectively see what people need and help them get those needs met.

There is always an opportunity for you to replace negative judgment with positive mindfulness. Develop the mindset of a leader. How you think in the heart of your mind will determine the behaviors you will exhibit. If your thoughts are negative, your behaviors will encompass negativity. The reverse of course is true. As you maintain positive mindfulness, your behaviors and actions exhibited will be positive.

There are several techniques to keep yourself "happy" at work. I will share my 3 top tips in this area but before I do, we have to discuss "happiness." First let me tell you that happiness is irrelevant. It is dependent on so many external influences. That's why it's elusive to so many people.

If you're working in a really dysfunctional workplace sometimes the only thing you can do is to leave it. Before you do, try some of these tips.

➢ Make sure you have your attitude together. So often it's easier to see the toothpick in someone else's eye but you can't see the tree trunk in your own eye. Take time to reflect on your own values and aspirations. Do they fit with the organization? Can YOU live with what you do at work? What's going on with your personal life? People who are miserable in their own life are often miserable at work.

➢ Live and let live. Just as you examine your own dreams and decide how you fit into the world and work, so are your coworkers. People come from all different backgrounds and experiences. Those experiences color the way we perceive the world and approach our work. Big eye opener... Everybody doesn't do things the way that you do and you can't live someone else's life for them. (Mind your business.) The good part is we all can learn and we all can change. We don't have to hold on to those things that don't work well for us or others.

➤ Don't fall for the "itching ears" practice. This is where you are the gossip carrier or "listener." Do you notice how bad news travels fast and positive information has a very short life? This is human nature. Try YOUR best to be the positive influence. Use lunch time and breaks to just talk. Absolutely NO gossip or work talk at the table. (This is Mandatory.) Be the transformer in your workplace. Lead the way. Everyone may not come with you but you will be happier when you are the captain of your own ship.

Finally let me restate that happiness is an outside job. Joy is an inside job. Joy is what you carry inside yourself based on your beliefs about your place in this world (purpose). Joy builds confidence and is not as easily influenced by outside forces. However you do have to protect it and nourish it. You do that by taking time for yourself. You can't' give what you don't have!

The Mindset Of A Leader

Your mind is where decisions, planning, focus and implementation begin. You need tools and strategies to get your mind on track. There are great tools for you to implement in your life so that you can *be* blessed and bless others.

Romans 12:2 (KJV)

And be not conformed to this world: but be ye transformed by the renewing of your mind, that ye may prove what is that good, and acceptable, and perfect, will of God.

The work that we do requires we manage our mindset closely. There will always be challenges, unrealistic expectations requested and difficult people. You will need to develop strategies to have ways to remember your purpose, remember your passion and remember what you are really working for. The world says it's money, fame and power. We also know you can't take any of it with you. So renew your mind with your reasons for being your best as often as you can in a day. It really does come down to moment by moment decisions.

How do you manage your mindset? I remember working at a facility where as a manager my responsibility had grown from managing one unit to managing five units. When a new VP arrived on the scene and said to me, "They said you're good but we'll see," I knew things could change and they did for the worse. Coming to work was becoming increasingly difficult. I had a choice each day regarding how I was going to respond to coming to work.

I could go in each day complaining about everything or I could go in and do my best for my staff and the company. I chose the latter. Because I had developed good working relationships with my staff, I continued to have some joy working with them decreasing my stress levels in many ways.

Mindset is the key to being able to do this. One way I managed my mindset was to each night, think of the things that went well that day. Did my meetings go well that day? Did I meet my goals that I set that day? Here's a good one. Is it me? Is there something I could have done differently or better? If the answer was yes, the next day I would adjust accordingly. If it was no, then I did NOT take on the burden that others tried to put on me. I remained thankful for the opportunities to grow in my knowledge in the area of healthcare where I was working. When you can be thankful you actually change the brain chemically. Endorphins are released and you get that "feel good" feeling. I rejuvenate my soul with music and I love to laugh.

Proverbs 17:22 (KJV)

A merry heart does good like a medicine but a broken spirit dries the bones.

Learn how to move on instead of holding on to foolishness. I bring my joy in the door with me in the morning. Since I love music, each day, I would go in singing songs from my favorite positive artists.

I may not always leave the way I came in but the next day, it's on again! Here's some strategies every leader needs to help keep a positive mindset as a leader.

➢ Organize your environment so it's conducive to decreasing stress by being clutter free.

➢ Identify and change habits and thought patterns that don't serve you.

➢ Take time for yourself. Watch comedies, inspirational or stress neutral shows like Home and Garden TV (one of my favorites).

➢ Listen to music with a message. Something light hearted and catchy. If you can, have music available to listen to throughout the day to help you stay focused on your joyful mindset.

You can increase your ability to find joy and fulfillment in your work and personal life. Your "why" comes disguised as your satisfaction in how you serve. What you focus on is what you will get more of. If your focus is on the negative things happening in your life, you will get more of it and your soul and spirit will become disheartened.

If you focus on keeping a merry heart as described, those joyful endorphins will keep you joyful and allow you to be inspired and creative in helping others. It's one of the benefits of being a Legacy Leader. Through music, thankfulness and a lot of prayer among other things I was able replenish my soul with positivity so that I could have something to give the next day. I was able to remain effective and have good outcomes for a long while. Eventually I did have to leave but I made the choice to reflect and take the lessons I learned to create a better work /life balance in my next job.

It's about balance. Managing your mindset is the beginning to creating balance between what your purpose is and how to manifest it effectively with power!

The best way to manage your mindset is to realize there is a balance that happens between selfishness vs altruism. There's a phrase 'a closed hand can't give or receive.' You became a leader because you wanted to and believed you could make a difference. If you think that your leadership is all about you then you are operating with a closed mindset. It is about you but it's not all about you. Attempting to create balance without mindful introspection and alignment of your mind, body, soul and spirit is difficult at best! Real leadership starts with you being able to lead powerfully from within.

Let's see how taking care of your body plays a significant role in living your legacy.

Body

We take care of our bodies so that we can serve without depleting ourselves.

I Corinthians 13:3

And though I bestow all my goods to feed the poor, and though I give my body to be burned, and have not charity, it profiteth me nothing.

Your body is important because it houses the mind, soul and spirit. Everything you do will be done in your body. Like a home that's not maintained well, it will eventually begin to have holes that let the elements ruin your foundation leaving you on shaky ground or leaks in your roof. We know all the diseases that can plague the body when just one electrolyte is out of balance.

Are you running around with your head spinning? Are you an expert at multitasking? That's a problem, not an asset. What do you do to take care of your body? Most of us work too many hours, get too little sleep or exercise and eat poorly. We are nurses! We all took anatomy and physiology. We studied how all of the organs work in harmony together for one goal. To keep you able to participate fully in this journey called life. We are wonderfully and fearfully made. As nurses we know there's a price to pay if we don't take care of ourselves. As the verse states, you can sacrifice yourself physically for the work of caring for others but the reality is without doing it with love for yourself and others, there's no benefit to you as a person.

Your Body Can't Give You What It Doesn't Have!

Your ability to be an effective leader will be compromised if you don't take care of your body! Our body provides constant feedback to us. Physical intelligence is the ability to listen to and acknowledge physical signals your body sends you.

When you eat at your desk and work through lunch, you don't make that mind-body connection. This is why so many of us fight weight issues. We usually don't eat the right things especially at work. Be mindful of your body. Look at how you eat. Are you really hungry or are you eating mindlessly? You won't be in good health if you continually eat poorly. It's also not acceptable to not eat lunch, or eat at your desk or on the run. Without adequate nutrition, your body will betray you by making you irritable, cloud your judgement and make you slower to respond appropriately to situations.

Nurse's bladder is when you don't even remember to go to the bathroom because you're just too busy. To not go to the bathroom also means we are most likely dehydrated. Too many of us have this problem. It is definitely not beneficial for our overall well-being. Having no life-balance has a major impact on your ability to be at your best. Self-care is not a luxury, it's a necessity!

I carry my stress in my gut. I also carry my intuition there. Stress will decrease my ability to be in touch with my intuition. Physical intelligence is when you listen to your body; you will know what's happening. If it's stress, who or what situation is causing it? Next step is to assess, "Am I causing the stress behavior? If so, what part did I play in this?" What can I do differently to change the dynamics causing the stressful situation?

A moment of mindfulness in your physical intelligence realm will de-escalate anger and other strong emotions that affect the body releasing cortisol and other hormones into the body. Taking a step back will also allow you to really assess the situation. Now the reality is you may not be able to do this right away but I am strongly suggesting that you do it before the day ends.

You won't feel energetic when you haven't had enough sleep. You don't sleep well if you have unresolved things on your mind. Develop relaxation rituals at night. Remove TVs, cell phones or stimulating conversation at least one hour before bed. Without proper rest and release of stress, you come back to work just compounding barricades to enjoyment and fulfillment. Stress continues to build and it just becomes a vicious cycle.

What is your body telling you right now? Your choice is to listen and to act on what you know and feel in your body. When you don't give your body what it needs, eventually it will not give you what you need. When you are mindful of your body, you can make the right choices for it. Physical intelligence is when you listen to and act on what your body is telling you. Develop the body of a leader – one that has stamina and clarity of thought.

Physical Environment

As much as I didn't want to admit it, I was wasting time. How? By not keeping my work environment organized. If your office, cubicle or unit space is messy, your mind may become disorganized also. The result of a disorganized mind is your actions will be chaotic in nature. I used to tell myself, "Messy is okay." I had a certain level of messy I was comfortable with. Papers would be all over my desk and yet I thought it was no big deal. At times I would need a specific piece of paper or item on my desk. I knew it was there and I thought I was locating it quickly. The truth is, it might take me a minute or two to shuffle a few things around before I actually located it.

What I later realized was that those extra few moments it took to look for that item was wasting a few minutes, here and there, several times a day. Those wasted minutes were adding up by the end of the day and even more by the end of the week. I was frustrated and wondered why I was working extra hours at the end of the day just to complete things that I didn't get to earlier in the day. I was wasting time day after day.

I began to do what I call, "Pick it up and handle it sort of day." This is where I do not allow myself to move things around. If I pick it up, I must handle it to its completion. It may not be what I wanted to do first but if I picked it up I must do it. By doing this I found that I really became more productive. For so many years we've been taught that multitasking was an essential skill. Now we know it may be more of a curse than a blessing. As managers we have so many things to do in a day. You have to prioritize and re- prioritize minute by minute. Organization is an important skill that will help you in you work life and your personal life. As you are organized, you will reflect a sense of confidence to those around you.

Soul —

3 John 2

Beloved, I wish above all things that thou mayest prosper and be in health, even as thy soul prospereth.

This is God's desire for all of us. That we prosper not only in material things, but also in health and in our soul. This indicates that care must be taken for us at an almost cellular level. That gut where your intuition lies. That part of you that knows there's more to life. Until you take care of yourself at this level, you won't prosper.

The real you resides in the soul. It's what makes you, YOU! The soul is the essence of you. We are influenced by our environment, our relationships and many other things in our lives, but there is a part of you that is what some call "the real you." That space is where the soul resides. The soul is what connects us, as human beings, to each other and to our higher spiritual self. Purpose lives and thrives in your soul. The desire for something more lives here also. You have gifts, talents and strengths that, when identified, can take your ability to affect positive change in others to a whole new level.

This is where your leadership in service comes into play. We are here for a purpose. We need to connect with our purpose and see our part in the big picture. Within that big picture we are here to connect as human beings. We are our "brother's keeper." We are ***privileged*** to lead. To lead from an unattached place is soul suicide. It kills the joy and makes us lose sight of our purpose. While you have breath, your soul is alive and needs to be nurtured.

You see, everyone has the God-given right to "prosper and be in good health even as the soul prospers[v]." The soul is also where authenticity resides. It's ground zero. What you feed *or* deprive your soul of, will determine how you manage and feel about yourself, your life and career. You have to build yourself up so you absolutely become and remain thankful to be alive in this day and time. Then you will have something of quality to give to others.

What you feed your mind definitely seeps into your soul. Ratchet TV is not the answer. What are you reading? Do you spend most of your time with people who are miserable, angry or always have drama in their life? If so, it's time for a change.

Set aside quiet time. Reflect in quietness. Our soul is the connector of our mind and spirit. Maybe have inspirational or relaxing music. Create a thankfulness journal and write something daily. What are you doing to nurture your soul?

Your Breath –

Sometimes we need to just breathe! Feel your breath. Take a few deep breaths right now. Attempt to slow it down. Hear your heartbeat. When you are in this space, can you listen to what your soul is telling you? Self-awareness is first. Paying attention to yourself is the key to effective leadership. You need to be in tune with all that you are and come from a place of alignment in your very soul. When you take time to really reflect mindfully and soulfully, you will find peace, joy and will be able to connect more with your purpose and others. Paying attention to and appreciating others will help you extend that peace to others who we have the privilege of leading both in your personal and professional life.

When your soul is in balance, your creativity, insight, intuition and choices you make will be operating on a higher plane. You will be aware of your impact on others and you will make the best decisions because you will relate to your mind, body, soul and spirit. You oversee your legacy! You have the control. The only chance you have to create yours is *now* while you have breath. What is your soul telling you?

Spirit —

Galatians 5:22, 23 (ESV)

But the fruit of the Spirit is love, joy, peace, patience, kindness, goodness, faithfulness, gentleness, self-control; against such things there is no law.

Though listed last it does not lessen its importance. As a matter of fact, it is the very foundation for everything that we are. It's the major ingredient in finding and living your legacy! It's what supports your morals, ethics and decision-making. Spirit is what feeds the soul and helps the mind put all things in balance. Without it, there will be a hole in your soul which will become larger, swallowing you up in all of the foolishness of the world that takes the joy from your work or life in general.

Keeping God in first place in your life is vital to servant leadership. If you need patience, if you have no joy (inside job) or have a need for self-control, here is where you will find the main source and support for these things. Without spirituality, you lose the ability to see the REALLY big picture of a world view and legacy view. It will be hard to sustain the resilience you will need to face the challenges of everyday life today creating results for the future.

As Maslow's theory suggests, self-actualization is where we are living our purpose. I suggest that self-actualization lies in and maximizes in the spiritual realm. Your purpose and your legacy really begin and end here.

You need all of the benefits of the fruit of the Spirit to lead powerfully from within. There's more than working, collecting things and having power. Spirituality is about a bigger plan that we are a part of...Herein lays our true purpose and legacy.

God knows the plans He has for you! (Jeremiah 29:11)

All cultures that have ever existed identified with a higher power outside of themselves. The spiritual aspects of life cannot be ignored. When you look at the grand Sequoia trees, beautiful beaches and fabulous mountains around the world, you know there's something more to our existence than just going to work each day. How and where do *you* fit into the scheme of life? Your value is even more than those trees and mountains.

The answer is, God has a purpose for why you are here. When your mind is focused and your soul and spirit are in proper order for you, everything falls into place. You can be peaceful in the eye of the storm!

In my desire to become an entrepreneur, my journey was filled with many starts and stops. For a long while, the interference in my business getting off the ground was working full time (or so I thought). I was able to decrease my schedule to part-time and I thought that would do it. Not! Well I finally was able to retire early and I said this is it now! Well not so. For the longest time I couldn't figure out what was going on. Though there were a few factors that were holding me back, one big one was that I was out of alignment in my spirit connection.

God does know the plans he has for you. That's why we need to check in to identify that plan. Your gifts and talents are just that, gifts. Check in with the Gift Giver for help getting clear on how to use them.

Developing the Spirit Within

The Spirit of God is what ultimately drives our love and our desire to help others ethically in service. We have to look outside of ourselves for a source of help, inspiration and motivation. Inspiration is ***in-spirit-action***. Inspiration doesn't just show up in our lives, you need to seek it out. You can't just muster it up. No matter what your level of spirituality is, you need to embrace it. You won't reach your highest potential without it. You can be the answer to someone's prayer or someone else could be the answer to yours. As for myself, this verse keeps me knowing I have help.

I look to the hills from which comes my help – Psalm 121:1

The inner you is comprised of your mind, body soul and spirit. We discovered the secret of using the practice of mindfulness to secure your sanity in the world of management. We see how physical intelligence allows you to listen to and act on what your body is telling you in order to be your best. We then examined the place where the real you resides…the soul. Finally we see a glimpse into the spiritual aspect of life where I believe real purpose begins and ends – the caring, the love of people the desire to help others reach their highest potential. After all, that's what we do for our patients. Next, let's put the pieces together and relate them to real time leadership situations.

SECTION THREE –

PRACTICAL LEADERSHIP

The Struggle Is Real

The role of the front-line nurse manager has become more stressful today due to the changing healthcare environment. Not only are some managers on call 24-hours, seven days a week, they are held responsible for their own clinical practice and the clinical practice of others even when they may not be there.

As healthcare becomes increasingly more complex, organizations must adapt to compete. The core responsibilities of the nursing leader are to assure delivery of quality, cost effective care, and management of the nursing practice including staffing, patient flow, staff/patient ratios and safety. Patient satisfaction, patient outcomes and cost containment: requires leaders to translate the strategic goals and objectives of their organization and have them realized at the organizational level.

Middle managers hold the key to the organizations real success, while studies show that they are some of the unhappiest workers. Middle managers often have to enforce policies that they did not develop to subordinates who might object to those policies. Middle managers endure the pressure to multitask more and more each day; yet, many nursing managers are not treated as one who holds real power.

Traditionally, in healthcare, nurses receive little credit for their contributions to the successful outcomes of their patients. Nursing leaders also receive little credit for getting the job 'done!' These things, among others, increase job dissatisfaction among nurse leaders and leads to apathy and decreased effectiveness as a leader.

Nursing managers can positively or negatively influence the accomplishments of a healthcare organization. As nursing leaders, we must transform ourselves by becoming knowledgeable about who we are and how **we** can work "Smarter not Harder" to be effective. We must also empower ourselves to ask for what we need and want so we can take care of ourselves, our staff and our patients along with implementing the visions of our companies and our profession.

So, How Come So Little Recognition?

I believe one reason is, we consider ourselves as nurses who are providers of care, not necessarily leaders. How can we lead powerfully in the healthcare community when we are not leading powerfully from within?

Hosea 4:6a
My people are destroyed for lack of knowledge

Lack of appropriate knowledge is a great place to start.

What Should Leadership

Look Like?

The essence of leadership is to live our lives in service to others, unselfishly (our definition), for the greater good. It's about having a passionate desire to influence people impacting them for the better, who will then influence other people, and so on creating legacy. In that sense, all nurses are leaders in the lives of our patients; that's why nursing is more than just a job for us.

God placed you here to invest your life in others. You have gifts and talents that bring a uniqueness to the world only you can bring. When you discover your passion, are clear about your purpose, and understand how to control your legacy, you will be effective in enjoying your life and impacting positive change on others. Effective leaders leave a positive legacy that lives on for generations.

First let's look at the dictionary's definition of the word 'leader'. Quite simply it means; *"a person or thing that leads, a guiding or directing head, as of an army, movement or political group."*

What I love about this definition is *"**guiding or directing a movement.**"* That's what we need to do as nurses – especially nursing leaders. We can lead a movement where nurses are coached, mentored, empowered, acknowledged and appreciated by all in the healthcare arena. Our goal should always be for us to all rise to the height of our own potential. As most of you know who are reading this book, that's just not happening enough right now. The real point is—the movement starts with you and can start right now!

To break it down just a little more, let's look at the word *"lead."* There are over 50 definitions for this word. For our intents and purposes I chose only a few.

➤ To go *before* or *with* to show the way.
➤ To conduct by *holding* and *guiding.*
➤ To guide in direction, course, action opinion etc.
➤ To *influence* or induce.
➤ To have the directing or principal part in.

The privilege of being a leader is that you have a positon of influence! You have the authority to make changes to any situation, however small or large. You have the power to make other people's lives difficult or easier, peaceful or chaotic. You have the power to make things happen.

To be truly effective you bring all of your resources, like vision, fortitude, patience, integrity and compassion to your position within an organization, so you can advocate for yourself and others. The power you have in leadership needs to be tempered with the reminder that it is a privilege.

The Privilege vs The Power Of Leadership

Whose Needs Are Being Met?

How often in our nursing career have we met those nurses and managers who are the "keepers" of information? Whenever you need to know something you must go to them. When you ask a question, they look at you with disdain as if to say "you don't know that?" Why? It's about power and control. You know the old story give a hungry person a fish, feed them for a day, teach them to fish, feed them for a lifetime. It's the same with knowledge. I believe you should share what you know especially if it will benefit that person. You will BE more powerful as you empower others to direct their own lives.

As nurses at the bedside or in the community, sometimes we tend to get into our nurturing mode. We want to care for our patients to the point where they are dependent on us. We feel needed. We teach them how to care for themselves but we just don't feel like we can discharge them because we wonder if they will be okay without us. Their situations are not as perfect as we would like them to be. Still we must let them go and live their lives with the information we gave them.

It's the same with our children. Helicopter parents who take on an over protective or excessive supervision of their child are examples of this type of staff supervision. Are we creating an environment for them to grow or remain dependent so we can feel useful?   This is one reason many parents suffer with empty nest syndrome when their children grow up.

As leaders, we need to guide and give information. Remember, what's the motivation? Are you meeting your needs when you train? Do you have the "need" to be "in charge?" Or are you willing to share the wealth, the spotlight so we all can be powerful! When managing your staff, try not to take things personally. You have to let go of control. Don't shut your staff down. Be open to the fact that they may have different opinions and ideas that can also bring value to the work of the company. There are consequences and responsibilities for all actions. We, as leaders, need to be accountable and hold others accountable also for the greater good.

Process vs Outcome

As a nursing leader, you are tasked with the productivity of your staff and you are tied to the outcome organizationally through raises and promotions. Some leaders believe this means they need to exert high levels of control to manage the outcome. These leaders usually feel the need to penalize when errors are made instead of learning from them because they feel defined by attaining that outcome. They see problems and solutions as *only* their own. Here's where that leader would benefit from looking within themselves to identify why they respond this way. It would benefit them by decreasing overwhelm and stress in their own careers and allow others to participate and realize their potential as they are challenged to grow both personally and professionally.

Your priority, as a nursing leader, needs to focus on the process more than the outcome. As a leader, we are responsible to define the process. The process is the how of what needs to be accomplished. If you focus on the process, you will be able to see gaps in knowledge, practice or policy which can direct your interventions.. However, a process must always be flexible enough to allow for individuality. You can collaborate in helping to find the solution and embrace the outcome. It doesn't become all about you or the individual, it becomes about the work to be accomplished. See, the work represents the bigger picture. The bigger picture, the vision, supersedes any individual – even you.

An effective leader will strive for the expected positive outcomes, always keeping the variables of the "people factor" in mind. Learning and growing is a process. Mistakes are inevitable. We can teach each other how to minimize mistakes and learn from them through analyzing, implementing and adhering to processes. On the practical level, when things go wrong, following the process will help you identify gaps in learning and practice of your staff. It will eliminate the need for you to be right.

When nursing leaders remain personally detached from the outcome and focus on the process they become better able to help other nurses without being emotional or reactive. When we do this, we will all be less judgmental and provide consistency for those we lead. The outcome focuses on desirability. The process focuses on feasibility.

Here's what we need to do to develop the next generation of nurse leaders:
> ➢ Teach insight.
> ➢ Develop resilience, (the ability to bounce back after setbacks).
> ➢ Teach value of self.
> ➢ Teach the mindset of service leadership.

We can neutralize our own agendas and judgements in the background of our decision making. Developing awareness and alignment of your mind, body, soul and spirit is key. Personal transformation and caring for oneself as a priority will create an environment where everyone can win.

How Is Your Leadership Manifested?

Do you ask yourself, why am I in this management position? I'm stressed and overworked. Most of my staff is making more money than me and yet here I am. The question is: How is the power and privilege of leadership manifesting in your life? What is your leadership looking like? Are you coming home mentally and physically ***exhausted*** feeling like you accomplished nothing? Do you feel like you carried all the weight of everyone's expectations evidenced by overwhelm and frustration? Are you questioning whether your daily work is even important anymore?

Stress is inherent in the nursing profession. Burnout is happening to the nurses in all areas of healthcare. It's also happening to our nursing leaders. Expectations of higher productivity, increasing demands to do more with less, the squeeze between staff and company goals enhance the stress our leaders feel. That stress makes for short tempers which can lead to episodes of disrespect and bullying which plague our profession. As leaders, we can and ***should*** change that.

If this is the case, your foundational philosophies about leadership are absolutely leaking your energy and your joy. If you consider that you are doing the best you can, it's possible your perceptions and beliefs should be examined. If you want to change the outcome, you need to look deeper into what may be an underlying need or challenge for you.   Just picture a beautiful vase with several cracks in it of varying sizes and depth. Any liquid you put in there will leak out, either slowly or quickly leaving you with nothing or much less than you put in. As leaders and as nurses we pour part of ourselves into others on a daily and sometimes hourly basis. We almost never ask for anything for ourselves. Keep doing this over and over on a daily and yearly basis, it's no wonder we burnout. If you don't replenish and 'overfill' yourself, you will become empty or have little to give.

Let's remember why we are here.   We, as leaders, *are* the ones who face challenges head on. We take the risks and can get the sense of fulfillment when we've coordinated a job well done.   We are the ones who offer our shoulders for others to stand on. So why are we shrinking from our responsibility as leaders? I believe it's because we don't realize when our reserves have become low or even empty.

Real success is when you live your life with a consideration and care for the *real* you (mind, body, soul and spirit). You can seal the cracks in that beautiful vase we spoke about earlier. That vase represents you. When you are intact mentally, physically, emotionally and spiritually, you can be filled to overflowing. Then, you can freely give out of the abundance you have!

What's Legacy?

Legacy is one of those words that are stuffed with meaning, but our generation has almost forgotten what the word even means. Why is the premise of legacy important? I believe legacy leaves an undeniable benefit for those who follow your lead. The essence of legacy is when you believe that your purpose is bigger than you. Legacy brings a weightier value to leadership.

You can live your legacy of leadership and enjoy it when you stay in touch with your inner you and your purpose – knowing first, that your impact on others is directly related to your ability to lead yourself. You can only effectively lead yourself when you align *your* mind, body, soul and spirit. You *can* change your mindset, direct your heart and skills, and get to the place of *loving* what you do wherever you are in your personal and professional life! When your life is in order, those around you will easily reap the benefits of your work without depleting you.

Legacy and Leadership

Legacy leadership is about intention. As nursing leaders in management, we have stepped into the leadership role desiring to make a bigger impact in our organizations and in our sphere of influence. Legacy leadership is a compelling way of *living* forward —a way of intentionally influencing people to have the results of that influence extend beyond a generation or two; As I have said before, "it's all about you but it's not all about you!"

When you think about it, *you* have been influenced by many leaders in your personal and professional life. Some have made a positive impact while others may have made a negative impact on your life. Even when people have made a negative impact on your life, you have the choice to change the perception from possible victim to victor. Sadly, some have made no impact at all. (They were neither hot nor cold.) Their life's interaction with you left no mark. When you really believe your life matters, you will decide to be hot and passionate about your life! You will touch someone's life for the better. Seek those opportunities. You may not even see the result right now but your intention to make a difference will cause a shift in the world for the better.

You have the *choice* to perpetuate what you learned from your relationship experiences with the nursing profession or discard it. Too often we hear "well I went through that and now they have to "pay their dues!" We can lead that movement of living to our highest potential and make mentoring an absolute part of our legacy to future nurses.

93

When I was a new nurse, I was usually given the worst assignments without a lot of input or help from the more "seasoned" nurses. I can remember seeking help and being made to feel as though I should know the answers already and by not knowing I must not be such a "good" nurse. I remember wondering how everyone seemed to get their work done and the charting and still leave close to the end of their shift. Yet as hard as I tried I couldn't get it done! Of course, in time I got better and realized some of the many shortcuts that were needed to accomplish this feat.

But then, the real lesson came as I saw new nurses come to the units, and they were given the same business that I had been given. There they were floundering as I had been with the same general consensus "I had to go through the same thing and I made it." "If they don't make it, maybe they're not meant to be a nurse." Now I just have to say here, that's some chicken head mentality and yet it's so prevalent in our profession.

What's missing? *Compassion and empathy.* Ask yourself how you would feel if you were bullied. How do we reconcile that kind of treatment to our fellow nurses and yet take the time to readily explain treatment protocols, the non-compliant, rude patient? We tend to turn off the compassion mode when we deal with each other. As leaders, we can set the tone and stop the madness! Make the choice to let your legacy leave a positive impact.

The way to begin living true legacy of leadership is to live compassion! Compassion for yourself will teach you how to care for others (The Golden Rule). True compassion for others will fuel your legacy. Always remember, there is at least one life waiting for you to mentor, to teach or to care for them. Your purpose may be to influence a staff member, patient or co-workers' life who their purpose may be to make a huge impact on the world. Effective leaders do not operate in a vacuum.

Legacy (Transformational) Leadership In Action

When we look at leadership we find there are many facets to it. We are all individuals bringing our own flavor and style to leadership. For example: As nursing leaders, we benefit from the legacy left by transformational leaders like Florence Nightingale[x], Captain Mary Lee Mills[xii] and Lillian Wald[xiv]. They had no idea at the time, how many lives would be touched by their leadership but they did have a purpose and vision that included wanting to make an impact on the lives they encountered. I'm sure they didn't go about their day saying, "What will I do to leave a positive legacy today?" They did, however, make a choice to live up to their potential. These women had vision, took risks and implemented their ideas to make things better. They also had the future in mind, evidenced by their willingness to teach others and share information. They were living transformational leadership.

Transformational (legacy) leadership is when you help pave the way for someone else. We need to work today with the future in mind. That's the vision. You prepare for transfer of leadership by actively sharing knowledge, wisdom and the power of your gifts and talents. The purpose of transformational leaders is to become the catalyst that brings people out of the darkness into the light. We must become that light first by transforming the leader within ourselves.

"Rather than just living day to day for the fleeting pleasures of here and now, a legacy-minded man or woman

96

deliberately considers life as a gift not to be wasted and all these really important things are 'invested' in the light of a multi-generational perspective." (Reclaiming Your Legacy)[xv]

Legacy leadership is when our *ability* and *will* to help others are in sync. Skills must match desire. However, despite popular opinion, this synchronization doesn't just happen. We need tools, direction and support to grow and *develop* our abilities *and* our will.

As a Legacy leader, we walk on the path toward self-actualization through creativity, independence, spontaneity and a grasp of the *real* world. Legacy is quite simply to leave proof that my life mattered and that I had thought, feelings, philosophies, something to share. When on this path, you will be living your legacy powerfully and in all its fullness. The outcome is peace of mind, soul and spirit.

So, what's the benefit of legacy leadership?

- ➤ Increased *personal power* and *confidence.*
- ➤ *Fulfillment* because you will understand and operate in your purpose.
- ➤ The ability to *enjoy* your work!
- ➤ The opportunity to make a difference in your life and the lives of others!

Three Qualities of Legacy Leadership

Character *grows from the seedbed of truth and inevitably stirs our desire to pass along what we've learned through the education of others.*

Education *is a life-long process of increasing transformation out of darkness into light. One of the most primary domains of education surrounds all the aspects of what constitutes our health and wellness, both materially and spiritually.*

Influence *is enabled by all the previous "pillars" that Providence has built into our lives and should clearly be an effective "platform" to establish a society-wide acknowledgment of the truth that is constantly at war with the deceptions and darkness that constantly tries to hide it (Reclaiming Your Legacy)[xvi].*

It's a Journey of Influence

Your brain commands your physical body. Your spirituality commands your soul. A healthy self-image is reflected by thoughts feelings and philosophies that impact you and your problem solving abilities.

In my journey toward maturity, connection to others and dealing with challenges, I realized that being connected with my purpose and leadership, brought transformation. Initially, I was a reluctant leader. I always had the heart of a leader but as a shy child, I didn't always step up to take the full package of what true leadership entails. Circumstances pushed me toward leadership.

When I was growing up, I knew I wanted a career but I was sure it would not be in nursing. My grandmother was an operating room technician and my mother was a Licensed Practical Nurse (LPN) who later became a Registered Nurse (RN). Both of my aunts (her sisters) were also nurses. In my infinite wisdom, I was not going to be a nurse.

When I was out of work as a young single mother, an opportunity arose for me to take a Home Health Aide (HHA) training course (I applied because I needed a job). Well, to my surprise, my heart and soul found its home.

Healthcare allowed me to rely on knowledge learned and refine precise skills i.e. initial anatomy, simple dressing changes and signs and symptoms. This was also when I began building my skills as an informal leader. An informal leader is when you are the one who people come to for information, advice, and direction or as a source of strength and influence. This may be in addition to and/or despite the presence of formal leadership.

That HHA program was not only a transition into healthcare; it triggered my drive to success and to help others succeed. It was a pivotal point in my transformation. I began helping my classmates with tutoring, sharing information and advocating so that everyone could pass the class and have the same opportunities. At that time, I discovered my reason for being, which was helping others.

As an informal leader, I was visionary in my purpose without being self-actualized. My goal was to inspire others to stretch and grow with support. You can still make an impact as an informal leader no matter what stage of self-actualization you are in presently.

While helping, others is one of the reasons most of us went to nursing school, it turned out to be the first place some of us learned about how difficult it could be experiencing relationships in the nursing profession. But here's the lesson: People who make it difficult for you in your journey also bring value, believe it or not. Once you examine the situations and circumstances and your reactions to them, you will have the opportunity to make a choice and grow from them.

I was influenced by my mother and aunts regarding what perseverance looked like. I was influenced by their desire to help others. I was also influenced by the negativity I found working with some of the nursing instructors and staff while in school; however, I chose to take that negativity and use it to inspire me to treat other nurses with empathy and compassion throughout my career. The journey of influence is just that, an ongoing journey of challenges, resiliency and growth if you embrace it.

SECTION FOUR

LEAD WITH POWER BLUEPRINT

Self-Care – Blueprint Care Plan

The "Lead With Power" Blueprint follows the concept of the care plan. The first step is realizing there is a problem. As we saw in examining how your leadership is manifested, there are symptoms that will show you that something is not working. Frustration, overwhelm, feeling persecuted are all signs something is not working. Assessment is the key. Next step is to design interventions.

The "Lead With Power Blueprint" steps are:

➤ **Introspection- Assessment.** Identify something is not working. How are you "showing up" in this situation? Controlling, overworking, retreating, frustrated? Is this behavior showing up elsewhere in your life?

➤ **Needs- Diagnosis.** Determine what role you are playing. Initiator? Victim? Recognizing you have a role is the key. We express ourselves by our behaviors. What story is your behavior telling you? Is that a fact or belief?

➤ **Intervention** strategies are to be designed according to your insights. The only changes we can make are with ourselves. The truth is, when we shift, so does everything around us. Keep your vision in mind. What needs are you trying to meet? What can you change?

Evaluate your mind, body, soul and spirit connection. Implement self-care. Here is where you identify and set up your support systems.

- ➢ **Adjust your thinking and perceptions** by choice.
- ➢ **Identify** your resources.
- ➢ **Develop** healthy boundaries.
- ➢ **Learn** how to build in reflection time to refresh the soul.
- ➢ **Develop** a continuum for mental, physical, emotional and spiritual intelligence.

The Struggle in Real Time – Using the Blueprint

Creating healthy boundaries is one of the struggles many leaders and individuals have. Boundaries are necessary both externally and internally. Examining our belief systems and perceptions will give us insight into why we may not be creating those necessary boundaries. Too often we don't have a plan so we're not sure what outcome we are looking for.

Without a plan, life can be a journey of meaningless tasks – things to do that don't have any sense of long lasting fulfillment. We become subject to the will and desires of other people or organizations. You can achieve a sense of purpose and *balance* using a tool like the "*Lead With Power Blueprint*" and live your *legacy* in the fullness of the present. Here is an incident where I learned aspects of the Blueprint experientially.

I was hired as a supervisor in a healthcare company. It was a high-energy position. It consisted of a lot of meetings, a lot of training along with policy and procedure updating. In addition to the business of the day, HIPAA (Health Insurance Portability and Accountability Act) was just being introduced and my company was part of the pilot. I had two huge 4-inch manuals that I had to read and integrate the HIPAA regulations into our policies and procedures. Well, I started out enthusiastic! I love a challenge as do many other leaders. After the business and meetings, etc. were done for the day, I would stay a little

105

later after everyone went home to try to keep a handle on my other duties.

Well, staying ½ hour per day initially helped me stay on top of everything. But soon it wasn't enough. ½ hour turned into 1 hour. Then 1 hour turned into two. Then I started meeting the office cleaning staff when they came in and before long I was saying goodbye to them when they left. After a while I was staying late enough to meet the night security guard. I was also not sleeping well. In my own world, I was just trying to keep afloat. Asking for help made me feel as though I would be perceived as weak. My enthusiasm persisted because I got the praise and recognition of being *"the woman!"*

The Problem

Everyone else was going home and not staying late. I was getting work done and apparently making my day job look easy because I continued to receive more responsibilities. Only me, the security guard and the cleaning people really knew how much time I was spending after work. Only me and God knew how I wasn't sleeping well. In my effort to keep on top of my job, I kept thinking of strategies on *how* I could keep up and still be wonder woman at work.

I started keeping a pad and pen at my bedside so I could write ideas down when they would come to me. The problem was ideas come just as you are falling asleep as the brain slips from conscious to subconscious. If your mind is too busy, you cannot sleep; thus you will not have good rest. I was not as sharp as I needed to be during the day. I was out of balance.

My family suffered because I wasn't home and when I was there, I didn't have much to give them as a mother and wife. Compassion for my staff dwindled also. Initially I believed everyone should do what I was doing to "give" more to the company. This work ethic influenced the way I perceived their work ethic. i.e. were they being lazy? Non-caring? I was out of balance.

The Realization

As you can guess, I began to burn out. I was stressed and running on fumes! I had given all my mind (thoughts), body (working long hours, not sleeping) and I didn't have any more to give. Eventually I was diagnosed with hypertension, had increased headaches and had a basically unhealthy lifestyle. I was not increasing my effectiveness as a manager, I felt unappreciated and for sure, I had lost my joy in leading my staff.

That saddest thing was when I tried to get back to normal balance and began to ask for help, I was met with lack of support from my leadership when I couldn't keep up the farce. In fact, I was chastised for not doing my work effectively! I couldn't dial it back successfully. I became a victim in more ways than one of my success!

But was it really success? We have chosen to be in an awesome position that impacts lives. I could not remain effective once I stopped taking care of myself. By placing my company, work and peers above my basic needs, I became frustrated, overwhelmed and unhappy.

After leaving that position, I took some time to reflect on what happened. I had to gain some insight to what subconscious needs I was getting met by going overboard in trying to accomplish everything as one person. I asked myself some introspective questions that form the blueprint. What caused me to not ask for help early on? What's my role or complicity in this problem?

What stole my peace and joy and the biggest question of all: Was this the outcome I was looking for?

I took some time after leaving that job to reflect on how poorly I was managing my mind, body, soul and spirit. I realized how imbalanced I had become. With introspection, I discovered the need that recognition held high value for my inner self. I had formed the belief that this recognition is best when it comes from others.

The problem with that belief is it puts me in a position to have my sense of being valued (through recognition i.e. promotions, congratulations, raises) in the hands of other people. Obviously, I had no control over what others thought or how they would act on any given day. When I had asked for help and was not supported, I felt unappreciated and devalued as an employee and yes, as a person!

Some other key insights were:
➢ I had contributed to the problem by not understanding how and when to say NO!
➢ I needed to set boundaries internally and externally.
➢ My inner desire to please others at my expense was a behavior based on old survival beliefs.

I lost the understanding of what really brings contentment at work, and the balance that was needed to keep me joyful in my personal life. (All work no play…makes Jill and Jack dull)[xvii]

I realized I was imbalanced in several relationships. I was not honest in the relationship with myself. I was over giving trying to prove my value as an employee by doing more work and not relating to the quality of the work I did. My relationship with my upper managers had no boundaries. I didn't set any. My relationship with my staff suffered because now instead of guiding them, I was depending on them for recognition. Lastly my relationships with my family suffered because I wasn't there physically or emotionally.

Discovering my thought patterns through introspection, I was able to develop an intervention strategy to help change those harmful thought patterns. What I kept was my work ethic but I balanced it with my new-found ways to give myself recognition and remembering I had to reconnect with my value as an individual and a leader. I learned to create healthy boundaries. I had to reprioritize the love I had for my family and their importance in my life.

I was successful in changing my mindset about obtaining and maintaining balance in my next leadership position. I still produced good work but no more cleaning people or security guards for me! No more sleepless night with pen and paper by the bedside. I might have to do a little overtime sometimes but now my strategies reflect how to work smarter and not harder by putting self-care first and setting boundaries. Guess what! It works! It can be done! You must love you, care for you, and enjoy you.

As noted in my story, many of the problems I was having were directly related to a state of imbalance in my mind, body, soul and spirit. Physical intelligence is one way to see the signs of imbalance. Headaches, stomach issues, difficulty concentrating or overthinking to name a few. Creating boundaries is essential in your work life and personal life. Develop insight. Take some of the inspiration you give to others and give it to yourself first. This perspective is found when you learn how to balance yourself.

Balance

Use your emotional and physical intelligence to see the signs of imbalance. Abruptness, overwhelm, anger and inability to sleep, to name a few. Creating boundaries is essential to the well-being of your mind, body, soul and spirit. This perspective is found when you learn how to balance yourself.

Here are some strategic ways to be a balanced leader.

- ➤ **Be Mindful of your value**. You bring value as an individual no matter where you are even if it seems like you have a small role. Always examine your why (purpose).
- ➤ **Look** at all the possibilities and variables that come into play in each situation.
- ➤ **Examine** and sometimes re-examine your own values to see how they fit into the big picture.
- ➤ **Take action!** Don't just sit around passively waiting for someone or something else to change your circumstances.

When balanced, you will be true to yourself. This is where you will find peace, joy and love. You get to give of yourself without coming anywhere near depletion.

The Courage of Advocacy

One of the benefits of tapping into your own personal power is that you get to be an advocate for yourself and others.

Being an advocate is a primary focus in nursing. We always think of our advocacy as related to our patients. We also need to advocate for each other and ourselves as these next few stories exhibit.

GUIDING PRINCIPLE #11

COMPASSION FEEDS FORTITUDE. COMPASSION IS A TENDER HEART TOWARD SOMEONE WHO NEEDS HELP WITH A STRONG DESIRE TO ALLEVIATE THEIR SUFFERING. FORTITUDE IS OUR ABILITY TO PUSH THROUGH THE HARD TIMES.

Patient Advocacy

As a LPN I was working in a small hospital and I had a patient on our step down unit who was suffering from what would later be discovered to be Stevens-Johnson syndrome. Her skin was literally falling off her body. We practiced team nursing at the time. The patient was on isolation of course and it took a long time to just provide physical care.

Eventually, as tasks often do take up so much of our daily lives, most staff didn't want to spend so much time to take care of her because it took time away from their other tasks. (The lesson here is don't get so involved in getting the tasks done that we forget about people as human beings.) I became her almost private duty nurse. I remember one day I was gowned up as usual head, mask, gloves and I was giving her a sponge bath because she was getting weaker and could no longer get in the tub, she said to me "I can see in your eyes you care." That solidified for me the meaning to "the eyes are windows to the soul." I did care.

Her condition kept declining and we couldn't figure out what to do. The talk on the floor moved to wondering whether she would die. Her physician was one of the most feared doctors in the hospital. (This was at a time during the 1980's when a doctor entered the nurse's station, the nurse had to get up and give them your seat. Can someone say power?)

I went to many staff nursing leaders and made recommendations for her care and asked them to follow up with my ideas. No one would do it for fear of overstepping their bounds with this doctor. I also was afraid to shine. Eventually, it was the compassion for this woman that made me get over my fear and advocate for her.

One day, after providing care to this patient, and being compelled to do the right thing, I went to her physician and told him what I observed taking care of her. That her condition was not being adequately treated by us, she was dying and she could better be served in a major hospital's burn unit because they could provide care to that type of patient where the skin barrier was compromised.

He actually listened and transferred her out. Many months later I was able to reconnect with her. She was healed and home doing well. That's why we do this! It is a privilege to serve with compassion. Someone else's needs at times are more important than your fears. This is the true meaning of advocacy.

Advocacy For Leaders

Staten Island, where I live and work, was one of the hardest hit places by Hurricane Sandy. During this storm, we had an emergency not only for our patients but for our staff as well. As managers, the amount of pre-planning was huge. We had to anticipate many scenarios and have executable plans for each. All the staff was busy but the level of responsibility was huge.

As a home care agency, we had to decide who needed to be seen, who lived in low lying areas (which were many) and what their evacuation plans were (if any). We had to reach out to all vendors – especially pharmacies – to make sure all patients had enough medications to cover them for a few days.

Then the storm hit and we found ourselves in even worse shape than we could have ever imagined. We had staff and patients in need of evacuation and some who found themselves homeless. Telephone service was sketchy at best and as managers we had to account for all our staff and patients. Many nurses slept in hospitals and nursing homes for days manning extra shifts until help arrived. Homecare nurses walked through flooded streets with downed electrical lines or drove as close as they could get to a patients' home and then walked to provide care. Some could work from home calling patients and their families to make sure they were okay. Emergency room nurses saw an increase in their census regarding people who had no support at home or became homeless from the flooding.

For my agency, we had one manager who almost single-handedly managed the operations for two days until things began to normalize. As a company, we took care of our patients. Even when things settled down, the nurse leadership team was in countless meetings and committees analyzing what had happened and how we could do it better. When it came time for appreciation and recognition again (as far as the public was concerned) there was very little shown for nurses. Our company, as well they should have, gave significant recognition for our nursing staff. The management team? *None.*

I have seen this type of scenario repeat over the years through many catastrophes in many different healthcare facilities. I felt compelled to take the risk and have the courage to bring this up to my CEO as she came out to congratulate the staff nurses for a job well done. We need to remember our leadership position is realized in first leading yourself. Bring your desire to create win-win solutions to any discussion of a problem.

If you feel strongly about something, get the courage to stand up and speak up. Come with solutions in hand. Advocate! It felt so unfair to me that the nursing manager who, without her dedication, we as an agency, would clearly not have been able to safely care for our staff and patients during that time, got no recognition. We need to stand up for each other!

Well here's the other side of leadership....my CEO; she listened. She opened the door for the company to embrace more opportunities for nursing leaders to have input and get recognition for their work. Through compassion for my peers and exercising the courage to speak up, teams were created, changes were implemented and managers began receiving tuition reimbursement, increased leadership training and an increased voice in determining workflows. Even though I am no longer at that agency, the impact made was lasting. That's legacy!

Advocacy for Self

As nurses, we often consciously/unconsciously accept the premise that our positions have little power. One area this is expressed has been in the arena of salary. Ranges differ from state to state in the United States Ranges differ depending on the area of work i.e. hospital, nursing home, clinics and home care. More sinister is the fact that there is an unspoken rule that we don't speak to each other about our salaries.

A situation occurred when I accepted a position and I thought I had negotiated the best salary. From then on it was standard company raises and bonuses. I did alright with raises and bonuses and never bothered to check if I was being paid fairly. Well about 4 years went by and in an open, honest conversation, I found out that a coworker was making more than me and didn't match my longevity with the company or my educational degrees.

This was the first time that I ever had evidence that I was being paid fairly. Without divulging my sources, I discovered that it was within my right to request a salary review. I decided to advocate for myself. I wrote to my Vice-President to discuss the process. It was confirmed and I did receive a pretty decent raise. However, they would not give me retroactive. Just think of all the money I lost probably for a few years. This taught me that you need to monitor your career closely in all aspects. In this instance advocating worked but in another instance it didn't.

Performance reviews can be an ardent feat for the reviewer and the reviewee. For several years my performance had been 4 out of 5 which I agreed with. Then one year with new management I was given a 3. When I questioned this assessment, I was told, "It went down because of the overall performance of the entire team." I was outdone. I addressed it and couldn't get anywhere.

My mistake was not advocating for myself timely or appropriately. I let her dictate as the end all and be all. I spent that whole next year angry and disappointed. That didn't make any sense. From that incident, I learned to never take no for an answer and not to procrastinate when advocating for myself. The passion and effort we use to advocate for others MUST be used for ourselves. We matter!

When it happened a second time I stepped up courageously. I went through the chain of command and was at the level of going to the CEO when I decided to leave the job. I never received the appropriate review but I felt great that I stood up for myself. We must be wise and vigilant in managing our career. It's easier to always see where others need assistance. We must become just as sharp for ourselves to see when we need the advocate.

Blueprint Tips

GUIDING PRINCIPLE- #12

PREPARATION IS THE HIGHEST FORM OF BELIEVING. YOU MUST BUILD YOUR ARSENAL OF INTELLIGENCE IN ALL AREAS TO BE PREPARED FOR ANYTHING. THAT INCLUDES FORMAL AND INFORMAL KNOWLEDGE ALONG WITH EMOTIONAL, PHYSICAL, AND SPIRITUAL INTELLIGENCE.

The tips in this section will complement the inner work you do with the ***Lead With Power Blueprint***. These are some of those organizational and personal tips that will help you navigate the world of leadership.

Set the Tone

My first position as a Director of Nursing in a home care agency had me ill-equipped to manage staff. As a new person, I heard a lot of, "I don't do that!" "That's her job!" Others would pull me to the side to say, "They did that for the last director" or "The last director did this." I learned quickly that I needed to set the tone for my own position and how I would handle issues. I learned that it is the most important factor for effective leadership that a leader sets the tone. This is true of new managers and seasoned managers who may be taking on new staff, or may just realize that what they're doing just isn't working.

The way you dress, keep your office space, speak and handle yourself professionally are all involved in setting the atmosphere in which you work. You set the tone of how change is accepted by yourself and your staff. You set the tone of how you will be treated by your peers and co-workers. You set the tone on how your staff will treat each other. One of my phrases is, "The fish stinks from the head down."

Three tips to help you set the tone at your workplace:

> - **Learn** your job description and your staff's job descriptions (if you have staff). If you don't have staff, know the job descriptions of the people you will work with closely. You really need to know

what everyone does so you can see how the different positions interact to form the big picture.

➢ **Survey** – Speak with and observe your upper direct reports, other managers, staff and ancillary staff to understand the culture of the organization. Every organization has its own unique culture. Sometimes different units will have their own sub-cultures. This is to avoid being a "bull in a china shop" or be "run over" by some bulldozer type personalities.

➢ **Lead** – Lead with confidence. Once you understand processes and culture; don't be afraid to implement new things. You are the fresh eyes and with due diligence most likely have very good ideas because you haven't been totally incorporated into the culture. Don't be afraid to take calculated risks or make mistakes. As long as you learn from them, you will continue to grow.

Initially, every job has a learning curve. When starting every new position, you need time to learn the policies, procedures, staff and culture of an organization. This is a major key to leading well. Some leaders come into a company and proceed to make changes right away. This usually wreaks havoc on the morale of staff. It also usually causes problems within the systems that are linked to many of those policies and procedures that are in place.

Enhancing the Blueprint Tips

Tip- as a leader you will help create a better transition of your leadership by learning your environment before acting.

Tip- Clear the clutter out of your environment. – Clutter leads to confusion and indecisiveness. Organizing your physical environment is a great beginning to help you get and keep your mind clear and your thoughts in order.

Tip- Take time for reflection. – All too often we are sooo… busy. We move from one task to another quickly without even thinking. Take time to think about where you have been for your lessons. Take time to think about where you are now so you can determine your vision and smell the roses. Take time to reflect on where you are going (vision). It is crucial to take time to cultivate your vision within your mind, body, soul and spirit in sync is crucial. Take time to refresh.

Tip- Take action! – Procrastination is the major killer of potential. We are all born with the potential to be great at something. By staying in situations where we are comfortable and not challenged, we slow our personal growth and end up not living the life we were meant to live. Take action! Stretch out. Start small but stay persistent. When one goal is accomplished, take time to assess, reflect and evaluate its impact on your overall life as you prepare to move to the next goal. Don't stop! See how your life will blossom and how living life becomes easier and more enjoyable.

Tip- Be compassionate to yourself if you decide leadership roles in nursing or any other leadership role is not for you. Everybody has a place; your passion will guide you. Remember, you will always be the leader in your own life.

Tip- Be authentic in your soul, this is a great place to begin the groundwork for legacy leadership. Evaluate and prioritize what's important to you.

Identify Your Personal And Professional Goals

- ➢ **Identify** your values and vision for your life.
- ➢ **Stop** giving less time to yourself than you do others.
- ➢ **Develop** an astute understanding of what's important to YOU.
- ➢ **Discover** your talents and gifts.
- ➢ **Build** your personal power.
- ➢ **Seek** opportunities to do the same for others.

Tip- Look for opportunities to mentor those qualities in others. Don't try to change someone's life in a moment. That's not mentoring. It's a process. It's developing those qualities of introspection, caring, competence, courage, commitment and compassion within you first, then in others so THEY can see them. That's balance in mentoring. Everybody won't get it so be prepared to let people grow at their own pace. Process and accountability will keep you aware and balanced to see the difference.

Tip- Every person thinks they're right. As a leader, be open to other's opinions and their way of doing things differently. Keep your eye on the big vision and ensure that others are clear about the vision also.

Proverbs 21:2.

Every way of a man is right in his own eyes,
but the Lord weighs the heart.

Tip- As you help others gain that insight, be ready for others to teach you insight into your own self.

Tip- Always remember you have choices. They may be difficult choices but you always have a choice. Keep in mind not making a decision or taking action IS a decision.

CONCLUSION

Relationships are what make the world go around. Managing relationships is key to creating situations where everyone in the relationship can walk away feeling valued and powerful in their own right. The only way to manage any relationship successfully is to first manage the relationship you have with yourself.

Managing the relationship with yourself is a priority if you want to live the freedom that personal insight will bring. To get that insight you must be willing to do the work of self-discovery. You must bring honesty, perseverance, focus and compassion to the table for yourself. We tend to be our worst critics. We find this in those moments of our self-talk. Our self-talk is governed often by our subconscious. It's based on beliefs that we may not even be aware of. That's why taking time for introspection is mandatory if you desire to live your absolute best life. A best life is determined by how you care for yourself first and the how you care for and serve others. The how brings us back full circle to negotiating relationships.

Nursing leaders must value the concept of self-introspection and service. They must prepare for and desire to make Legacy Leadership a movement. The way this movement will happen is when you decide to live your purpose on a passionate level in your position as a nursing leader. We must have a healthy understanding of the value we bring to the world using this knowledge to push ourselves in the direction of self-actualization. Practicing and teaching mindfulness along with emotional, physical and spiritual intelligence will create circumstances that will shift to the positive. When obstacles to our growth occur, we want to assess whether our strategies to overcome them are survival or success strategies.

Discovering your purpose is not enough to make you an effective leader. You need certain skill sets. The common ones of good communication, patience, collaboration and critical thinking will transition you to more effective leadership. Adding empathy, healthy boundaries and organization among others in the *Lead With Power Blueprint* will increase your effectiveness in leading yourself. Marry your clinical knowledge with business savvy. Demand your expertise be respected. Whether you are seasoned or new to management, understand that leadership is a position of tremendous responsibility and accountability along with service. Your position is one of influence, privilege and power that can be shared with others to assist in their transformation to becoming powerful women and men.

Most of all, remember the most important value you bring to the table. YOU! Bring all of the fullness of yourself, untethered by your past or obstacles that come your way. Seek to be your highest self for the betterment of the world! You are that SPECIAL! Live your legacy every single day. Self-awareness, humility, empathy and authenticity will take you a long way on your journey to building your legacy.

Coaching and mentoring will help diminish the unspoken mantra "nurses eat their young." That's what I do as a coach. Teach and develop insight. Coaching and mentoring are my passion.

Remember you are the catalyst for change. You can change the culture of your office, unit, hospital or agency. You can balance your personal and work relationships that are unbalanced in your life. You have a powerful leader inside. When you change, everything will shift. To truly transform your leadership within, insight is one of the best tools you can have to help you integrate and reconcile your mind, body, soul and spirit.

Let's agree to stand together as nursing leaders! Developing the next generation of nursing leaders will depend on how we develop ourselves. You have a choice in how you live your life. You have choices in the way you work in your nursing career. Balance the power and privilege of leadership. Choose to intentionally leave a positive legacy that will change people, who will change people. Let's Do It!!

Are you ready for Success, Joy, and Fulfillment?

It's Your Journey and It's All Connected!

About The Author

Naomi D. Jones RN, MS, CRNI is a Registered Nurse, Life & Success Coach, Mentor, Author and Inspirational Speaker. She is known as the Life Coach RN. In 2005, Naomi started her own company, Consults Unlimited Inc. because she wanted to help nurses live and work smarter not harder! This desire led Naomi to develop specialized, coaching programs in Leadership, Personal Development and Career Management for nurses.

Nursing Career

Surprisingly, nursing was not her first choice for a career. Naomi started out as a Home Health Aide when nursing "captured her soul." She then went on to become a Licensed Practical Nurse and then an RN obtaining her Masters of Science Degree in Health Administration. She is also a Certified Registered Nurse in Infusion (CRNI). She has been in the healthcare field now for over 38 years with over 20 years in management. Naomi also served as a Lieutenant in the Army Nurse Corp Reserves.

Coaching and speaking are Naomi's passion. She believes that we should all strive to be transformational leaders from within. As leaders, we can enjoy building our legacy now and be effective in changing the lives of others. Naomi is happily married to Jeff for over 30 years, and is the proud mother of four and grandmother of four.

Coaching Philosophy

Everyone has the God given right to *"prosper and*

be in health even as the soul prospers." As everyone oversees their own life, at times, we need to "get out of our own way" to make the best decisions. As we develop our mind, body soul and spirit, we can see our choices clearly. Helping people overcome obstacles and find success by transforming themselves is a foundational principle of her coaching business. Naomi has served her community and profession as a member of many organizations over the years.

*"**Leading Powerfully From Within**,"* is Naomi's debut book which will expound the principles of leadership abilities, being a catalyst and the follow-through on living and leading a self-directed life by helping others. Naomi is co-author of two books, *"Second Chance Living: Out of the Darkness into the Light"* and *"You Can Become a Professional Nurse."* Naomi is a blogger and has written articles for *Advance for Nurses, Nurse Together* and *The Six-Figure Nurse.*

Contact:
Naomi D. Jones
Website: http://www.lifecoachrn.com/

Get Committed!

If you're ready to personalize your own blueprint or you want to know more about the ***Lead With Power Blueprint***, contact me at www.LifeCoachRN.com for a no cost 30 minute session.

Thank you for allowing me to share.

End Notes

---

[i]

(http://psycnet.apa.org/?&fa=main.doiLanding&doi=10.1037/h0086006)
[ii] Maslow, A (1954). *Motivation and Personality*. New York, NY: Harper. ISBN 0-06-041987-3)
[iii] Interview for *Beautifully Said Magazine* (2012)]
[iv] (Krueger) 2016

[x] http://www.biography.com/people/florence-nightingale-9423539
[xii]

http://www.nursingworld.org/FunctionalMenuCategories/AboutANA/Honoring-Nurses/NationalAwardsProgram/HallofFame/2012Inductees/CaptMaryLeeMills.html
[xiv] http://www.biography.com/people/lillian-d-wald-9521707
[xv] http://www.reclaimyourlegacy.com/home/
[xvi] http://www.reclaimyourlegacy.com/
[xvii] Old Proverb